IT HAPPENED IN
GLACIER NATIONAL PARK

It Happened In Series

IT HAPPENED IN
GLACIER NATIONAL PARK

Vince Moravek

TWODOT®

GUILFORD, CONNECTICUT
HELENA, MONTANA
AN IMPRINT OF THE GLOBE PEQUOT PRESS

A · T W O D O T® · B O O K

The publisher gratefully acknowledges the valuable assistance of Annie M. Beaver, developmental editor for this book.

Library of Congress Cataloging-in-Publication Data
Moravek, Vince.
    It happened in Glacier National Park / Vince Moravek. — 1st ed.
        p. cm. — (It happened in series)
    Includes bibliographical references and index.
    ISBN: 978-0-7627-1028-7

    1. Glacier National Park (Mont.)—History—Anecdotes. I. Title. II. Series.

F737.G5M67 2005
978.6'52—dc22   2004059930

Manufactured in the United States of America
First Edition/Fifth Printing

Contents

Preface

You can compare Montana's Glacier National Park with other parts of the world—Switzerland, Alaska—but ultimately the true splendor of the place cannot be put into words. It has to be seen, smelled, and breathed.

I stepped off the Empire Builder train in 1986 to report for "Red Bus tour guide" duty and was immediately hypnotized. As a "jammer," a term derived from the rough "gear jamming" required to operate the relatively primitive transmissions of Glacier's historic fleet of open-topped buses, my fascination for the place grew. During my time there I heard plenty of amazing stories and was inspired by the setting and the marvelous history of the area to investigate further. It's an honor to share some of Glacier's inspiring events and fascinating personalities.

The happenings collected here are only a fraction of the true, living history of the place we call Glacier National Park. From encounters with wildlife to the annual attempts to remove snow from Going-to-the-Sun Road to a quiet fireside talk with the famous Charlie Russell, Glacier holds an open invitation to visitors to become part of its magnificent heritage.

The Day a Mountain Fell
• 2,000 Years Ago •

The following account is based on a legend told in the Blackfeet tribe. Although we'll never know, it's possible that the landslide described in this tale was indeed witnessed by Glacier's early inhabitants. It would have been a thunderously dramatic event, and the spectators and their fellow tribal members were likely scared of the spirits who had given such a powerful demonstration of strength.

"Do you think the bear has tired? Perhaps it is finally gone." The whisper came from one of the two Indians who remained after the vicious and lightning-fast attack. The bear was nowhere in sight, which was not necessarily comforting. They were amazed to be alive; four others in their party had not been so lucky. One of the two survivors had been seriously injured, however. His left arm had been torn nearly out of the shoulder socket, and he was coughing up blood. As he lay there on the side of the mountain, laboring for each breath, he suspected he didn't have the stamina to make it down the mountain.

The other young Indian had escaped relatively unscathed. Nevertheless, he had a deep sense of foreboding, fearing that the beast hunting them was not yet gone. He could feel it out there in the forest, coming for them. Both men had sparks of panic in their eyes: They knew rival warriors could be fought, but they feared this bear could not. The only fast escape the uninjured man could think of would require leaving behind his friend, and that he wouldn't do. Yet he knew they could not stay where they were much longer.

The sun was dropping and would soon hide behind the far peaks. The last yellow rays filtering into the forest depths created countless shifting shadows. The small woodland creatures rustled leaf and branch. From his vantage point on what would one day be called Red Eagle Mountain, the uninjured Indian looked out across Upper St. Mary Lake. The valley was stunning, full of dizzying colors, and the surrounding rugged mountainsides were scarred by the dramatic results of centuries of glacial sculpting. He tried to formulate a plan for taking his injured friend home, but the falling darkness and lurking bear did not bode well.

Just then, a hulking shadow materialized out of the brush, made its strange, wet, huffing challenge, and loped straight toward the braves. Perhaps it smelled blood—or fear. The men couldn't run any farther, and even if they could have, their warrior's code dictated that they try to make a stand. Unfortunately, they did not have a clear plan or time to do more than react.

Whispering grateful prayers to his ancestors and thanking them for the years of grace and fortune he had enjoyed, the uninjured brave stepped out from behind the nearby boulders before consciously realizing his decision. He moved forward, armed only with a long knife and courage, to face the giant bruin that had stopped twenty paces off to lurch up on its hindquarters. The bear towered over the brave like a shaggy, black thunderhead.

Without warning the unimaginable happened. A devastating wall of rock, timber, and debris roared down the mountainside and swept the creature away. The earth flowing past the men filled all their senses. They could not explain what they had witnessed, for it was like nothing they had ever experienced before. Millions of tons of rock had become a flash flood, and half the mountain had simply fallen away. The force of the slide threw the uninjured brave clear over the rock pile and into the brush beyond. He managed to crawl, bruised and battered, to a safe spot to wait for the tremors and dust clouds to settle. Astounded by what they had experienced, the two men passed the night on the mountainside. At dawn they staggered toward their home camp. They could find no explanation for what they had seen and thus believed that protective spirits had rescued them from the bear. It was many years before another party dared go near the site.

This engaging legend incorporates both the natural history of the park as well as the human history. In most cases geologic time calls to mind the slow grinding of plate upon plate or the molasseslike flow of glaciers. Nonetheless, there are those events that happen in the blink of an eye and change the face of the earth forever.

The powerful glaciers that carved Glacier National Park accomplished their spectacular work from three million to twenty thousand years ago. The impressive landslide that scarred the lake side of Red Eagle Mountain, however, is estimated to have occurred just a few thousand years ago, a mere blink in geologic time. Scientists ultimately attributed this slide and others in the area to the Lewis Overthrust, a major smashup of continental proportions that happened an estimated one hundred million years ago, when giant chunks of the earth's crust were slowly shoved eastward from the Pacific, only to smash head-on into the North American continent. Over time the crash forced up the western mountains, with the unusual result of shoving older rock layers up and over much of the younger rock. Thus, Red Eagle Mountain consists of rocks more than one billion years old that overlay Cretaceous stones, which are barely one hundred million years old. This unstable platform is the basis for the legend "The Day a Mountain Fell."

Grinnell's Single Shot
· 1885 ·

This is more impressive—stupendously, almost unbelievably beautiful—than any view to be seen in
the whole length and breadth of the Alps. And as
for Yellowstone Park, compared with this part of
the Rockies, it [is] merely flat country!

—Dr. George Bird Grinnell to James Willard Schultz,

Blackfeet and Buffalo: Memories of Life
among the Indians

It was a glorious fall day in 1885, sunny and crisp, and James
Willard "Apikuni" Schultz was leaning back on a tree, his hat
pulled down over his eyes. It felt good to let the warm sun
seep into his bones—he knew it was one of the last chances
he had to feel truly toasty until the next spring. Many winters
spent in northern Montana had taught him to catch the warmth
and try to store it, bringing it out again on those days when the
sun didn't shine and the mercury dipped below zero. Again.

Eventually he heard the creaks and moans of the mail
stage coming down the road; he stood up and brushed the dust
and leaves from his pants and settled his hat on his head. A
man descended from the stage coach, fit and trim and of
medium height, in well-worn clothes much like his own. He
was Dr. George B. Grinnell, conservationist and editor of *Forest and Stream* magazine, and he hoisted a canvas-covered
bedroll, a war sack, a Sharps .45-caliber rifle, and a fly rod as

he strode over to Schultz. Schultz grinned: This was not the bookworm editor or Washington bureaucrat he had placed bets would appear. Relieved, they made their introductions, saddled up, and headed off for one of the most historic forays into Glacier Park that any writer or conservationist ever made.

A few mornings later, Schultz and Grinnell were joined by Yellow Fish, who was the son of a man who worked for the American Fur Company and a Pikuni woman, and they set out with a team of horses and a wagon to make camp in the St. Mary Lake country. Grinnell had come to Montana to document the area, hunt, and then return to Washington with animal trophies for the Smithsonian, and he was eager to get into the wild. The going was tough because they were attempting to pull the wagon over a game trail and had to stop frequently to cut aspen trees to widen the path. Nonetheless, they eventually got their wagon into the flats that separated the upper and lower lakes and made camp a few hundred yards below the upper lake.

On the second day of the expedition, the men went hunting. The day before they had climbed Flat Top, aptly named by Schultz in 1893 for its long, flat expanse, and Grinnell had shot a mountain goat, but the meat had been "too tough and musky flavored to eat," according to Schultz in his book *Blackfeet and Buffalo: Memories of Life among the Indians.* With stomachs rumbling, they were more determined to find meat they could eat and decided to begin their hunt on the mountain just to the south of Flat Top. Climbing up the slope and following game trails, they saw plenty of signs of deer, elk, and grizzlies but no other big game. Schultz wrote, "We had not gone far when, a couple of hundred yards ahead of us, a lone bighorn ram bounced out from a depression in the shale and went leaping swiftly on; at a distance of about three hundred yards he stopped, turned sidewise and stared at us, head proudly up, his perfectly circled horns, like washtubs, carried as though they had no weight at all. No more had it stopped than Grinnell brought his heavy rifle to his shoulder, quickly sighted it, fired, and the ram made one high leap, plowed down into the shale, and was still."

It isn't easy work to butcher an animal on a mountain and haul the meat back to camp, but the three hungry men did the job willingly. Later that evening, while the trio feasted on broiled fat ribs, they relived the finer points of the day, as men around campfires have done throughout the ages. Relishing the shot that found its mark even at such a tremendous distance, Yellow Fish cried out, "Oh, *Ho, Hai!* . . . he did not kneel and rest his gun; just stood and aimed it, and with one shot killed the very far-off bighead." And so they named the mountain Singleshot, in honor of the shot that saved them from going to bed hungry for the second night in a row.

That episode marked the beginning of Grinnell's influence on the naming of many of Glacier's most notable features. Sometimes the names were chosen for obvious reasons, as was the case with Divide Mountain, which is the dividing ridge between the rivers that flow to the Atlantic and Arctic Oceans, and Goat Mountain, where Grinnell, Schultz, and Yellow Fish encountered an abundance of mountain goats. Gunsight Pass, Gunsight Lake, and Gunsight Mountain were named for the V-shaped notch that is the summit of the pass, and Mount Citadel was so dubbed for its spired summit. In other cases they chose names based on people they wanted to honor, as is the case with Grinnell Lake, Grinnell Glacier, Grinnell Mountain (these three were named by Schultz, not Grinnell), Little Chief Mountain (the Pawnee nickname for Grinnell's friend, Captain Frank North), Almost-a-Dog Mountain (a Pikuni friend of theirs), and Mount Reynolds (Grinnell's assistant editor at *Forest and Stream*). And with a nod to his very first hunting trip at Glacier, Grinnell and the other members of his party named Fusillade Mountain for a hunting expedition in which a reported twenty-seven shots were fired at a band of goats, yet not a single animal was struck.

Grinnell and Schultz had become acquainted through a professional relationship. Schultz was a contributor to *Forest and Stream*. In the winter of 1883–84, Schultz asked Grinnell to use whatever clout he had in Washington to help save the Pikuni Indians. In his book *Signposts of Adventure: Glacier National Park as the Indians Know It,* Schultz reported that during the previous winter, the buffalo herds had been exterminated and the tribe had had to rely upon the populations of antelope, elk, deer, rabbits, and grouse on their reservation, but by fall even those were gone, and the tribe began to starve. It took months for Grinnell to accomplish much, due to the red tape in Washington and the slowness of travel, but in February Grinnell's wagonloads of food finally arrived.

This was only one of many times Grinnell advocated for the tribes. He was well known and well liked among the Indians he met, and they honored him by naming him, just as he honored the land he loved by naming what he found. He was called Gray Clothes by the Gros Ventre, Fisher Hat by the Blackfeet, White Wolf by the Pawnee, and "wikis," which means bird, by the Cheyenne, who noted that his comings and goings in the area were like a seasonal migration.

Grinnell's affinity for all things wild seems to have begun at birth, when he was given the middle name Bird. As a youngster he attended school at John James Audubon's home in New York and continued his studies at Yale, where his academic record left something to be desired but his passion to be a naturalist was unmatched. He went on his first dinosaur dig in 1870 and then served as the expedition naturalist for General George Custer on his trip to the Black Hills in 1874. These trips resulted in Grinnell's continued study of paleontology, and in 1880 he earned a doctorate in the field. Shortly thereafter, he assumed the editor position at *Forest and Stream,* the leading publication at the time for sportsmen and naturalists. He used the magazine as a forum for exploring the problem of diminishing game populations and disappearing habitat, thus sparking a national awareness about nonrenew-able natural resources. He also devised the notion of the game-warden system that was financed by small, equal fees from all hunters and managed by the states. This was a radi-cal departure from the undisputed and unregulated right-to-hunt that had reigned over the country until that time. One enthusiastic reader of *Forest and Stream* was Theodore Roose-velt, who worked with Grinnell to end what they saw as federal neglect of Yellowstone Park, as well as excessive commercial-ization there. Grinnell's conservation philosophy was the foun-dation Roosevelt used to build the American approach to conservation.

Grinnell's interest in the park was not simply to hunt there and bring specimens back to the Smithsonian in Washington, D.C., although he took that role seriously. Nor was he there simply as an anthropologist performing an academic exercise, meeting Indians and living somewhat as they did. Grinnell, perhaps foreseeing days when the nation would boom and ex-pand in all directions, wanted to preserve this incredible cor-ner of the earth for the animals he so admired. Of all the things Grinnell did to shape our nation's natural heritage, perhaps the finest was this: He was one of the three commissioners to sign the treaty with the Pikuni in 1896, acquiring the mountainous part of their reservation, which later became the remarkable corner of the earth known as Glacier National Park.

John Stevens, Hardy Engineer

· 1890 ·

> It was almost impossible to build and keep a fire
> going, so I tramped a track about 100 yards in
> length and walked it back and forth until enough
> daylight broke to make it safe for travel.
>
> —Colonel John Stevens, in a letter about his
> Great Northern solo expedition

John Stevens, a rugged engineer working for the Great Northern Company, was on the verge of something monumental. If he made it through the next few hours, he was sure he'd be able to accomplish what no one else had: He would find passage through the high mountains of Montana and map a direct overland route for rail use.

The Stevens expedition was not grand by any stretch of the imagination. For most of his journey through the mountains, Stevens had been alone except for his guide, a Flathead Indian employed to take him up a branch of the Marias River. By the time he and his guide had arrived in Glacier, winter was setting in. The accumulating snow and the mud underneath it posed a serious problem for the two men since they were traveling on foot. As the days passed, the weather worsened, and soon the pair were being battered by a fierce blizzard. The Indian guide argued for stopping and holing up, but Stevens was determined not to return to his employer without more information about how to reach the west side of the mountains. Leaving his fearful (but perhaps more rational) guide behind, Stevens continued on alone.

Just before nightfall, with both the blizzard and his strength waning, Stevens reached the pass and recognized it for what it was—a way over the Continental Divide! He had found it! Unfortunately, the feelings of success and satisfaction were short-lived because he wasn't at all certain he would survive the night to report his discovery. He knew that trying to trudge through the snow back to his guide during the night would probably spell his doom, so he reluctantly decided to stay on the pass until daylight allowed for a safe trip down the mountain. Alone and unable to find sufficient dry tinder, Stevens faced temperatures plunging to forty degrees below zero.

The engineer kept himself alive that long, lonely, frigid night by tramping back and forth along a 100-yard track. To keep his mind off his freezing toes, he played word games in his head. In particular Stevens found the genesis of the name of the Marias River a bit amusing. The nearby river was so named by Meriwether Lewis as he passed through on a trip rather akin to the one Stevens was making, although Lewis's was certainly on a more epic scale. Lewis and others on the famed Lewis and Clark Expedition were responsible for naming many of the rivers and passes in the West, and by the time they reached western Montana they had used the names of several prominent Washington, D.C., politicians and were moving through the ranks of their family members. Marias River was named for Lewis's cousin Maria, but the apostrophe was misplaced over time, turning Maria's into Marias. Stevens doubted the cousin would be pleased. But for Stevens, he was glad it had happened since it gave him a springboard for creating similar name games to pass the time as he paced back and forth in the snow, trying to keep his blood pumping.

When dawn finally broke, Stevens wearily made his way back down the mountain and into the annals of history. Stevens's employer, James J. Hill of the Great Northern Railway Company, was ecstatic. One of Hill's major goals had been to find the straightest and most direct route to the Pacific Northwest from Minnesota. The Great Northern line began as an expansion of the St. Paul, Minnesota & Manitoba Railway Company (SMMR), of which Hill became president in 1882. Originally the SMMR was called the St. Paul, Minnesota & Pacific, but because there weren't any actual tracks going to the Pacific, the name was changed. Hill and his business partners worked to improve service, upgrade equipment, and expand the range of the lines. Over the years many people had so doubted Hill's efforts to find rail passage through the mountains that they had dubbed his idea "Hill's Folly." With groundbreaking news of a usable pass and a new route for the Great Northern, Stevens quickly turned the folly into "Hill's Triumph." The pass was named Marias Pass, and by 1891 Great Northern rail cars were chugging up and over it. The new rail line eventually traveled 150 miles at a main grade of only 1 percent.

The result of Stevens's determination and derring-do not only benefited the Great Northern Company, it also made Glacier Park more accessible to tourists. In the early days of the park, several roads went up into the mountains, but the rugged peaks of the Continental Divide precluded any cross-park auto travel. After the opening of Marias Pass, however, motorists who wanted to travel from east to west and vice versa could do it by boarding a train and strapping their vehicle to a Great Northern railroad flat car. Finally, in 1933, the Going-to-the-Sun Road was completed, which enabled visitors to drive from one side of the park to the other without the inconvenience and expense of boarding a train.

After Stevens's discovery of Marias Pass, the Great Northern Company hoped Stevens could repeat his feat, so they sent him farther west to find a route through the Cascades. Though unable to find a viable overland route through those rugged mountains, he did discover one usable pass that still bears his name: Stevens Pass.

Stevens played a critical role in another national triumph when he responded to President Theodore Roosevelt's call to take over the catastrophic Panama Canal project from the French. Stevens used his engineering genius to implement practical, logical plans for the canal's construction. His innovative lock system took the place of unworkable plans for a sea-level canal. Stevens's dedication to the project didn't stop there. He was the first to take a humanitarian approach to the canal workers. Recognizing yellow fever as a serious threat, he provided employees with immunizations. The last case of yellow fever among workers was reported after Stevens's implementation of the immunization program.

A decade later, Stevens assumed leadership of Woodrow Wilson's 1917 American Advisory Committee of Railway Experts to Russia, improving the Trans-Siberian and Chinese Eastern Railways and even becoming president of the Inter-Allied Technical Board in Manchuria. He continued to gain accolades for engineering contributions throughout his career and even during the twenty years after his official retirement.

At present U.S. Highway 2, the main highway from East Glacier to West Glacier, is called the Roosevelt Highway. At the top of Marias Pass, the highway passes a huge stone monolith in honor of Theodore Roosevelt. The only statue at that site, however, is of John Stevens, a hardy engineer who helped bring the Great Northern to the northwest and consequently allow thousands of tourists to enjoy the wonders of Glacier National Park.

Although Stevens is credited with "discovering" Marias Pass, he probably wasn't the first person there. There's plenty of anecdotal evidence to suggest that many American Indians and mountain men used the pass, but none of them put a name to it or marked it on a map. Explorer Major Marcus D. Baldwin had observed the pass in October 1889, fully three months before Stevens, but didn't actually set foot on it and never recorded his discovery. Such historical technicalities might have been moot had Stevens been a little less hardy, for the roving engineer almost lost his life in the attempt to find a way through Glacier's gigantic, looming mountains.

Slips and Trips
·1905·

The woman never even said thank you for getting her out of the glacier.

—Frank F. Liebig, Forest Service ranger

Ranger Frank F. Liebig was about a quarter of a mile from the edge of Sperry Glacier, setting up his tent for the night, when he noticed a crowd of people gathered around a crevasse in the glacier. "There is the ranger now!" he heard someone shout, and two of the men in the group immediately raced over to him. They quickly summed up the situation, informing the ranger that a woman had fallen deep into the crevasse and that they didn't know how to get her out. In an attempt to find help, a third man had set off to get ropes, but the closest hotel was 10 miles away, and he couldn't be expected to return until the next day. The group left behind had racked their brains trying to figure out a way to help the poor woman, but they weren't even sure she was alive. With no useful supplies and no experience, they were as stuck at the top of the crevasse as she was at the bottom.

Liebig quickly forgot about setting up his camp for the night, turned his horses loose, and grabbed two lash ropes and an ax. As he and the would-be rescuers ran toward the crevasse, Liebig stopped briefly to cut a stunted green fir tree about 4 or 5 inches wide and 5 feet tall. He asked the two men to carry it, and the trio continued toward the glacier and then crossed about 250 yards over the icy surface to the crevasse.

As Liebig and the two men arrived at the scene, a few men were standing at the place where the woman had fallen in, and several other men and women clustered nearby, fearful for the woman below and anxious to participate in the daring rescue. Liebig cautiously crept over to the lip of the crevasse and peered down. The crevasse was shaped like a V, with a 5-foot-wide opening that narrowed slowly until the sides came to-gether about 35 feet below. The woman had fallen about 30 feet, and as she had dropped into the point of the V, her body had become wedged in the icy blue crack. She was not mov-ing, and Liebig figured she was dead.

Nonetheless, Liebig quickly set to work. "I selected a place on the lower side of the crevasse and set the green post into the hole and packed ice all around to make it fairly solid," Liebig wrote in 1944 in a letter describing the incident. He then tied the two lash ropes together and tried to create a good hand hold by tying a series of knots in the rope. When he was sat-isfied with the security of the handhold, he carefully tied the rope to the post he had stuck into the ice moments before. He then gave strict instructions to the men around him, telling them to hang onto the post so that it couldn't slip out of the ice. Finally, he threw the rope into the crevasse.

Grabbing the rope, Liebig lowered himself into the cre-vasse and slowly began to work his way down into its depths. The icy sides were slick and smooth, and there were no ledges or grooves for him to stand or crouch upon. When he reached the woman, he tried to pull her free, but the force of her fall had allowed her body to slide deep into the crack and lock into place. He couldn't move her without letting go of the rope, but if he let go of the rope, he wouldn't be able to stand. Finally, Liebig concluded he would have to lie next to her, send the rope back up to the men at the top, and have them send down the ax he had brought from camp. Once he had the ax, he "chopped a hole on each side of the ice big enough to put my feet in for a hold, then sent the ax again to the top. When the rope came down again, I started to pull the woman loose and nearly pulled her arm out, she was wedged in so tight." Eventually, Liebig was able to wrench her free from the icy grip. It was difficult work to hoist her up from the crack and maneuver the rope around her waist in the dark, cramped space, but finally he managed it; the men above them pulled her to the surface. When the men lowered the rope back to Liebig, he was frozen and too weak to pull himself up. He had to tie it under his arms so that he, too, could be hauled to the top.

By this time someone at the top of the crevasse had lit a lantern and candles. Everyone knew that the first, and perhaps most difficult, step of the rescue had been completed but that the woman still needed to be taken where she could receive some type of care. This would be no easy task in the dark, but a group quickly formed to do just that. Led by a man carrying the lantern, several others carried the woman down a narrow, rocky trail with a sheer drop-off on one side. Picking their way down the slope in the dark, the rescuers made painstakingly slow progress. Finally, they decided it would be quicker and safer to just lower the woman's body down the side of one of the cliffs. One man went ahead to receive the body below.

"When the body was half-way down," wrote Liebig, "the woman began to spin around and hit her head on the rocks, cutting quite a gash in her head, which must have brought her to. Because she let out an awful yell, which scared us half to death, as we had all thought she was a goner for sure. Then she fainted again."

At last the men finally reached a camp. Feeling victorious and still astonished that the woman was alive, the rescuers lit a big campfire and drank hot coffee and brandy to celebrate. Even the woman had several cups of brandy and was soon "gloriously drunk." The next morning a doctor was located, and he announced that she would survive the incident, though she surely wouldn't have, had she been in the ice much longer.

Frank Liebig had numerous adventures and close calls in the park in his thirty-three-year career as a ranger. His time at Glacier began in 1902, when he traded his German citizenship for American citizenship, quit his job working for an oil company, and began prospecting in the Belly River territory. Shortly after that he was offered a job as a ranger working out of Lake MacDonald at a wage of $60 per month. His patrol territory was unimaginably vast: the area from Belton to the Canadian border and from the North Fork eastward to the Blackfeet Reservation. He patrolled the entire area now designated as Glacier National Park, which comprises more than one million acres. C. W. Buchholtz's book, *Man in Glacier,* reports that Liebig was told to "look for fires, to keep the main trails open, to prevent the stealing of timber, to keep squatters and game violators out, and to turn in his daily reports at the end of each month in order to get paid. Then his supervisor gave him a double-bitted axe, a one-man crosscut saw, and a box of ammunition and told him to 'go to it and good luck.' " Clearly, rangers were expected to solve whatever problems arose with clear thinking and creativity, as Liebig did in this tale. Even without training in search-and-rescue techniques, such as checking vital signs before manhandling bodies and using gentler methods to return a victim to consciousness, Liebig saved the day.

Bull Head Lodge
· 1906 ·

If its [sic] laying down you need Lake McDonald is
the best bed ground in the world and my lodge is
open and the pipe lit for you and yors [sic]. You
know that Lake country sings the cradle song to all
who lay in her lap.

—Charles M. Russell,
in a letter dated June 17, 1918

Charlie Russell stretched out his legs and let the heels of his
cowboy boots thump down onto the rug. He squinted his eyes,
took his time looking around the hotel lobby, and sized up the
crowd. "I reckon I know just the story for you folks," he said,
looking both pensive and a bit pleased with himself. He was
seated by the huge stone fireplace at what is now known as the
Lake McDonald Lodge, under the watchful eyes of a trophy
moose mounted on the wall. Night was falling, and the van-
ishing light outside made the lodge's lobby, speckled with light
from the fire, feel more like a home than a hotel. About twenty
people were passing through the lobby, some of them headed
to the dining room for dinner while others returned to their
rooms after a day outdoors.

The thud from Charlie's boots hitting the floor was the
only introduction he required to begin addressing the group.
He didn't care if the hotel guests stopped to listen, but he knew
from experience that most of them would. "I've been around

these parts most of my life, and a fair amount of that I've spent with the Indians. A fella can learn a lot from them. One thing I learned is the power of a good story, and this one is a gem. But the only fair way to tell it is the way I first heard it. So for this story, you can't just use your ears. You got to use your eyes, too."

And after a short pause and a slow breath, Charlie began. He didn't utter a sound, just swooped his arms low and long. And then a woman's voice was heard. The folks in the audience hadn't paid much attention to the woman sitting on the other side of the fireplace as they listened curiously to Charlie's little speech. Many people didn't know who he was, so the circle of listeners was a bit slow to grow around him. But the people who did recognize him were quick to grab a spot in one of the chairs scattered around the fireplace, settling in with pleasure. After just a few sentences, it became apparent that the woman, whom they later would learn was Nancy, Charlie's wife, was interpreting Charlie's story, which he was telling in the sign language that was common among many of the Plains Indian tribes.

It was a lovely tale of a small tribe in eastern Montana. Charlie's hands moved eloquently through the air, rings glinting in the firelight, and Nancy's voice carried across the lobby, describing the struggle to survive during the harsh blizzards of winter, as well as the beautiful days of summer and triumphant buffalo hunts. Finally, Charlie's hands settled on his lap, and Nancy's last words floated across the crowd.

"Who are they?" whispered one of the men in the audience. "That's America's greatest cowboy artist," replied another man, who had been on his way to dinner when he saw Charlie positioning himself in his chair by the fire. "His name is Charlie Russell, and I don't know what he does better, paint or entertain."

In the summers of 1904 and 1905, Charlie and Nancy Russell visited what was then a forest reserve but would one day become Glacier National Park. It took one long day's train ride and a 4-mile wagon ride to reach Lake McDonald from their home in Great Falls, but to the Russells the trip was well worth it. Charlie and Nancy were among the first tourists to the area, and they realized they had found a special place—so special that in 1906 they built a cabin at the south end of Lake McDonald and spent every summer there until 1924.

Over the years the fame and popularity of both Glacier and Charlie grew, and in certain ways each was able to draw on the reputation of the other. In 1914 John Lewis, a former professional baseball player who had become something of a fur trader and land speculator by the early 1900s, constructed a grand hotel on the north shore of Lake McDonald. The Glacier Hotel, with its soaring lobby, became the place to see and be seen, with Charlie Russell as the primary local celebrity. Lewis did all he could to capitalize on the popularity of Charlie, from having the Russells announced as they entered the dining room to displaying Charlie's art in the lobby to providing Nancy with a guest cottage for use as a gallery.

Charlie found that this honor, while encroaching on his privacy a bit, was good for business as well as good fun. The "gallery" space that Lewis provided was an important private place from which Nancy could wheel and deal over Charlie's art. And there were plenty of prospective buyers to talk to: A handful of private homes were scattered around the shores of Lake McDonald by this time, and they were usually rented by affluent doctors, lawyers, and industrialists who either had some interest in the art of the West or had friends back home who did. Even if Nancy didn't make a sale while these visitors were at Lake McDonald, she often had a second opportunity at art shows on the East and West Coasts, where they frequently met these folks again.

One of the ways Charlie thanked Lewis was by performing a sign-language skit with Nancy, or sometimes with his friend, the author Frank Bird Linderman, in the hotel lobby. Charlie had picked up a little Piegan through the years, but he was much better able to communicate with Indians by using some of the sign language common among the numerous Plains tribes he had encountered. His vocabulary was fairly large, but he was by no means fluent. He didn't need to be fluent for these hotel shows, however, because no one there knew the difference; moreover, these demonstrations were carefully scripted and rehearsed, so he and his partner knew exactly how the presentation would go each time. Charlie's customary garb of high-heeled cowboy boots, tight trousers held up by a vividly colored Mexican sash, a plain blue shirt, and a Stetson rakishly tilted to one side must have completed the picture nicely. His hands were typically bedecked with at least three or four rings, which no doubt added to the beauty of the display. Charlie, always the storyteller, enjoyed these presentations so much that sometimes he and Nancy would repeat them at fancy gallery openings in Chicago, New York, and San Francisco.

Charlie had another unofficial role at Glacier, and that was as the storyteller on Howard Eaton's pack trips. In July 1915 the Russells took their first pack trip through Glacier with Eaton, the founder of the nation's first dude ranch. On these trips Eaton escorted his guests from St. Mary, on the east side of the park, up and over some of the most gorgeous passes in North America and down to Lake McDonald. Charlie, always easygoing and personable, loved these trips not only for the scenery and inspiration they provided but also for the chance to talk with Eaton's guests about the good ol' cowboy days of the Wild West. Seeing how much the guests loved to sit around the fire with America's premier cowboy artist, who happened to be a fine spinner of yarns, Eaton invited Charlie to come along as often as he wanted. The writer Mary Roberts Rinehart met Charlie on one of the Eaton trips and was captivated. In her book *Through Glacier Park in 1915,* she reports that Charlie was the "campfire star." "To repeat one of his stories would be desecration. No one but Charley [*sic*] Russell himself, speaking through his nose, with his magnificent head outlined against the fire-light, will ever be able to tell one of his stories," she related. Small wonder Eaton kept inviting Charlie to come along.

While Charlie relished the roles he found he had with Eaton and at the hotel, for him the real reason to be at Lake McDonald was always the beauty and inspiration he found there. Because Charlie and Nancy had purchased the land for their cabin before Glacier gained national park status, they had an "in-holding" that allowed them to build their private cabin and spend their summers within the park's boundaries. Charlie and Nancy were thankful for some of the protections that came when the area officially became a park, such as the ban on hunting, but it was somewhat bittersweet for them to have to share their special place with tourists.

Their cabin, Bull Head Lodge, was located about a quarter of a mile up the beach from Apgar and was named in honor of Charlie's logo, a buffalo skull, which he drew next to his signature on his paintings and sculptures. The Russells further claimed the spot as their own by erecting a large buffalo skull on the side of a tree that was near their boat landing. The "lodge" was little more than a rustic cabin with an outhouse, although the Russells remodeled and added new rooms as the years passed. There was a serious lack of privacy, for there were no walls between the various sleeping areas, but screens were placed between the beds to at least block the guests' views of one another. These screens were also the Russells' guest registers: A summer's worth of visitors all signed their names on the same panel, often adding droll sketches by their names; the next summer, all the guests would sign their names on a different panel.

Both Charlie and Nancy were fond of entertaining and being with friends, but this was particularly true of Charlie. He loved to tell yarns, waxing nostalgic about the early days of cowboys in the West, but he had other ways of entertaining his guests as well. For example, when Charlie had visited the

Southwest, he had learned a bit about pottery from the Hopi. Finding suitable mud on the shores of Lake McDonald, Charlie modeled buffalo, elk, horses, and Indians with tepees and tiny bows and arrows. He baked the figures Hopi-style to create miniature dioramas, which he placed around the property, especially along the coves of the stream that ran near the cabin. Combining two of his talents at the same time, Charlie liked to tell stories to his guests while he sculpted a small moose or coyote from a piece of clay in his pocket. At the end of the story, he'd produce a near-perfect replica of the animal, without ever having taken his hands or the clay animal out of his pocket. He was also quite fond of fanciful woodland creatures, such as elves, and he gleefully crafted the little folk from cedar scraps and moss and left them on the porch railings and steps to peer out at guests.

Charlie passed away on October 24, 1926, at sixty-two. He spent the last summer of his life at his beloved Bull Head Lodge, hoping it would be spared when a nasty forest fire roared through the area in August. The lodge was spared, but Charlie had suffered from too many health problems himself to live to see old age.

Race to Glacier: Last of the Glidden Tours

· 1913 ·

The White Men Are Coming! America's newest and grandest scenic playground awaits you!

—Print ads for Glacier Park, 1913

Louis Hill, Great Northern Railroad magnate, was witnessing his dreams coming true. It was 1913. Glacier had finally been designated a national park three years before, and the Great Northern had claimed the "Crown of the Continent" as its very own vacation destination—the best in America. Grand backcountry chalets had been constructed. Massive log hotels had been raised and would be expecting guests that summer. If all went according to plan, Hill's Glacier Park Hotel in East Glacier would be the gateway and centerpiece, surpassed in quality only by the spectacular natural beauty of the park, grandeur no human hand could hope to match.

For Louis Hill the party was about to begin—at least for now. By the time Glacier Park Hotel was ready to open on June 15, 1913, Hill had marketed the park through every medium within his imagination. Magazines and newspapers were flooded with grandiose advertisements. Multiple publicity stunts were staged. But in what many people consider his greatest promotion, Hill personally stepped in to revive the old

Glidden Tours with an offer to support a nine-day, 1,245-mile automobile race from the Twin Cities to Glacier.

Though called a "race," the Glidden Tours were more of a contest of endurance than speed. New England telephone magnate Charles Glidden began the tours in 1905, establishing a trophy for the winner of an annual long-distance automobile race. The American Automobile Association was a partner in devising and conducting these tours. As well as demonstrating the capability and durability of the newfangled horseless carriages, the Glidden Tours underlined the need for better roads in America. Americans were learning that cars were proving practical, but only if they had decent roads on which to travel.

At first only stock vehicles were allowed on the tours. Time limits were established for different classes, but speed alone did not determine the winner. Lateness, damages, and time taken to fix repairs (certain eventualities due to the rugged routes of the time) were assessed point penalties. Soon the tours were taking place in both the Northeast and the Midwest and were dominated by professional factory teams interested in competing with one another and using the resultant publicity to show off their products.

The factory teams, however, didn't find much value in the old adage, "There's no such thing as bad press," especially when failures, misfortunes, and misadventures garnered significantly more press than the actual winners. Eventually, public interest waned. As roads began to improve, state by state, and as cars became more reliable, the news from the tours stopped feeling new. By 1912 plans for a Detroit-to-New Orleans rally had been abandoned, and the Glidden Tours faced extinction.

Then Louis Hill stepped forward, planning one last run and a grand-slam promotional event for his favorite fledgling national park. Thus was born the 1913 Race to Glacier, last of the great Glidden Tours.

Only the most savvy of present-day automobile aficionados would find any of the competing cars familiar. Entries included

Metz roadsters, Krit runabouts, Hupmobiles, a Marmon, Premier, Little, Moon, Chalmers, and Locomobiles. To start the grand tour, twenty-five autos rolled out of Minneapolis on the rainy morning of July 11, 1913, including a Packard driven by Hill himself. Hill drove part of the day and then quietly returned to St. Paul. A Mitchell Moose ran out ahead as a pilot car, using a load of confetti to mark the route. The participants, depending on the class of vehicle, drove 15, 18, or 20 miles per hour. All cars were required to check in at control points established along the route at the noon hour and in the evening.

The first day was a rainy, mud-caked fiasco. Nearly every car ended up in a ditch on the way to Alexandria, Minnesota. Even the pilot car slid off the road and through a fence 5 miles east of Osakis. With the help of a team of horses, it was back on the road forty-five minutes later. This must have seemed like poetic justice to those persons who doubted the usefulness and viability of a horseless carriage.

The second day's pit stop was Fargo, North Dakota. True to form, the pilot car again crashed into a ditch. According to the *Minneapolis Tribune,* the occupants managed a "marvelously narrow escape from death in four feet of water." The third day was spent in Fargo, preparing for the challenging 188-mile leg to Devil's Lake, North Dakota.

As the days passed, the weather improved. So did the contestants' moods, especially as towns welcomed participants with raucous band concerts, impromptu parades, and scores of local cars joining the caravans for short stretches. By design the race route paralleled the Great Northern's railway line, and Louis Hill made sure the Great Northern maintained a lavish accompaniment for the drivers and press corps by running a luxurious hotel train along the route. As the *American Motorist* reported, the train gave "those participating every advantage of hotel comfort in the midst of the great open country." Hill indeed had pulled out the stops with two diner cars, an observation car, six sleepers, and a "portable garage" unit packed with every mechanical repair tool and part imaginable. There was also a newspaper car complete with photoengraving and postal centers and a linotype machine, which allowed reporters riding along with the tour to print their four-page daily, the *Glacier Park Blazer.*

After driving for days in bumpy, dusty conditions, a dramatic "ambush" outside Poplar, Montana, provided a welcome adventure for the drivers. A huge group of mounted Blackfeet in full battle dress swooped in to surround the unsuspecting motorcade, blasting off rifles and belting out war whoops. Fortunately, the startled drivers broke into wild smiles when they recognized that under the fierce war paint and costume, the "chief" leading the mock attack was a grinning Louis Hill.

The tour concluded after a final leg from Havre to Glacier Park Station in East Glacier, a distance of a little less than 200 miles. With great pomp and circumstance, race officials presented seven cars with perfect-score awards. The American Automobile Association Touring Car Trophy went to the president of the Duluth Auto Club, Dr. James D. Park, and his 1909 Locomobile. Mrs. Frank A. Witt of Detroit, the only woman driver in the tour, who alternated with her husband in piloting a Krit runabout, won another award. The coveted Glidden Cup went to a manufacturer's three-car team of Metz roadsters.

Throughout it all Hill was on cloud nine. He had a troop of tourists headed straight toward his hotel, with newspapermen in tow to spread the word about Glacier and the hotel, once they got there. And what a spectacle awaited them all. Hill had instructed his assistant to pull out all the stops to ensure that the festivities would be unforgettable, as well as reported by all the journalists following the cars. Hill's assistant didn't disappoint. A band played heartily as the cars chugged into East Glacier, and the drivers feasted on an authentic western barbecue dinner. At the end of the night, fireworks illuminated the sky. For some people in the crowd, including many of the Blackfeet who came to observe, these fireworks were the first they had ever seen. The whole event was particularly gratifying for Hill, who had encountered a few obstacles in reaching his dream of building the finest hotel on the east side of the park.

Originally, Hill's plans had been slowed substantially because, contrary to popular belief, the hotel isn't within the park boundaries but instead is located within the limits of the Blackfeet Reservation along with the rest of the town of East Glacier. Because of the already existent, thriving tourist activity on the park's west side, the eastern location was the only part of the park not staked out and claimed when Hill set out to build his lodge. Midvale, East Glacier's original name, had only one hundred residents at the time and served as the only convenient park access point along the Great Northern main line.

Despite the emptiness of the area, the Department of the Interior snubbed Hill's attempt to buy any land for his hotel. He was informed that there was no land for sale because no acreage had been set aside as a hotel site within the original town plan.

Hill would not be dissuaded. He called in some personal favors and persuaded Montana senator Joseph M. Dixon to push a bill through Congress that would allow him to buy 160 acres of reservation property. The bill passed in February 1912.

Though the bill set the price at $25 an acre, the Indian agent in charge refused to sell the property for a penny less than $90 an acre. Hill immediately launched a clandestine media ruse, publicly hinting that he was considering an alternate location just outside the reservation and arranging a secret "public protest" whereupon area residents would flood Senator Dixon with angry telegrams. When Dixon presented these threats to the Department of the Interior, the price lowered to an acceptable $30 an acre.

Hill instantly contacted St. Paul architect Samuel H. Bartlett. He also set about ordering the blueprints for the impressive building built for the 1905 Lewis and Clark Centennial

Exposition in Portland, Oregon, which Hill wanted as a model for his grand hotel. In March 1912, the E. G. Evensta Company of Minneapolis began staking out the site. Finally, Hill's dream hotel was on its way to becoming a reality. And with the arrival of the Glidden tour drivers and their entourage, the hotel would be christened in a stately style.

The wave of tourists who arrived in Glacier by motor car caused unanticipated consequences for Lewis Hill. Though motorists brought unprecedented press coverage to Glacier, which was a boon to Hill and his hotel, they also marked the beginning of the end of the age of rail dominance at Glacier. Within a few decades passenger rail service to Glacier was no longer a viable revenue source for the Great Northern, and the company eventually lost its hold on the hotel and chalets. But for the short term, Hill's plan to focus the nation's eye on the Crown of the Continent and its beautiful Glacier Park Hotel worked like a charm.

The Giant Grizzly of Gunsight Pass

·1915·

> The grizzly was as large as a horse, eating huckle-
> berries on the side of Mount Jackson and in the
> company of a little black bear.
>
> —Charlie Russell, report of supposed
> first sighting, with the Eaton Party in 1908

The Gunsight Lake Chalet was a marvelous backcountry refuge. Smack-dab in the middle of paradise, it served as one of the crown jewels of Glacier Park. Yet it didn't last more than a couple of seasons.

Some people say it was destroyed by the frequent avalanches at its Gunsight Lake location, whereas others maintain that it fell victim to the "Giant Grizzly of Gunsight Pass," a bear of mythological proportions that refused to allow human trespassers into his high-mountain meadow territory—or perhaps it was a combination of both.

Few photographs exist of this backcountry chalet, but the ones that do clearly show a substantial two-story structure. The 1913 *Superintendent's Report* notes the generous dining room and accompanying dormitory. No further annual reports make mention of the chalet, and it's generally believed that an avalanche during the winter of 1913–14 obliterated it. For some reason it was built right in an avalanche chute, not to mention the territory of a giant grizzly.

The chalet system at Glacier National Park owed its existence to Louis Hill, the president of the Great Northern Railway. It took only a few years—from 1910 to 1913—for the railway company to construct the Glacier Park Hotel in East Glacier and nine backcountry chalets or groups of chalets. Named for their geographic locations, the chalets were at St. Mary Lake, Sun Point (also called Going-to-the-Sun), Sperry Glacier, Granite Park, Cut Bank, Gunsight Lake, Two Medicine, McDermott Lake (now Swiftcurrent), and Belton (now West Glacier). Eight of the nine chalets were accessible by boat or trail only, but the chalet at Belton could be reached by train or car.

The hotels and chalets were a comfortable day's horseback ride apart. Though Hill wanted people to arrive at Glacier via his railway, his vision was that people would travel within the park by horseback. This was the only practical viewpoint, as the Going-to-the-Sun Road wouldn't be completed for another twenty years. In 1925 more than 10,000 park visitors toured the area by horseback, usually spending ten or more days in the backcountry. Many tourists who saw the park this way were accompanied by Howard Eaton, the founder of America's first dude ranch, located in Wyoming. Eaton would often spend summers at Glacier, guiding enthusiastic riders from chalet to chalet.

The Great Northern, however, was unapologetically focused on the railroad business, not on building and managing guest accommodations. According to Bridget Moylan's *Glacier's Grandest: A Pictorial History of the Hotels and Chalets of Glacier National Park,* Louis Hill remarked in 1911, "We do not wish to go into the hotel business; we wish to get out of it and confine ourselves strictly to the business of getting people there, just as soon as we can. But it is difficult to get capital interested in this kind of pioneer work." In the end the chalets were a financial drain as well as a managerial headache for the

Great Northern. During both world wars the hotels and chalets were closed, and over that time many of the chalets saw irreparable damage. Furthermore, as more and more people were able to see the park by driving over Logan Pass, interest in spending an extended stretch of time in the backcountry waned. The St. Mary, Cut Bank, and Going-to-the-Sun chalets were demolished in the late 1940s, and the Two Medicine chalets closed their doors in 1953. The chalets at Belton, Sperry, and Granite Park were sold.

Although the Gunsight Lake Chalet was in operation only for a short time, the highlight of a stop there was a trip to Blackfeet Glacier, which at the turn of the century covered about 5 square miles. Gunsight Lake itself was found at the juncture of Fusillade Mountain, Gunsight Mountain, and Mount Jackson. It's unknown whether or not any attempt was made to rebuild the chalet in a more auspicious spot near Gunsight Lake. According to former National Park Service director Horace Albright, there were efforts to maintain some kind of structure in place of the chalet, but the new structure was destroyed by a bear in 1915. Legends persist that this was the last skirmish with the infamous Giant Grizzly.

Historical records conflict: When was the Gunsight Lake Chalet destroyed, and how? It is most likely that the chalet was wiped out by an avalanche during the winter of 1913–14. But not everyone believes so. The Montana Historical Society has on record a single cryptic article from an unidentified newspaper dated December 27, 1929, with a rather sensational headline: "Giant Grizzly Roams Glacier National Park, Defying Man and All Efforts to Kill Him." The text reports the story of a mule packer in charge of transporting provisions from Sun Camp—a horsepacker's camp used as a way station for the packers as they worked—to Gunsight Chalet in 1915, a year after the chalet's supposed destruction by avalanche. The packer reported encountering massive bear tracks, "too large to be covered by his ten-gallon hat."

Later that same season, the packer noticed that one of his mules was missing. A subsequent search turned up a single blood spot and more huge bear tracks leading up the side of Citadel Mountain, in the northern part of the park. Near the timberline the packer found the meager remains of his mule.

A few days later, the remaining mules feeding close to the chalet were suddenly startled and ran into camp, crowding around the packer as if he were their mother. Along with a saddle-horse guide who happened to be in the camp, the packer went out on a scouting trip. He thought a black bear had spooked the mules, and he intended to drive the bear into camp for the amusement of the tourists.

It was not to be. Instead of a black bear, he spotted a giant grizzly in the meadows on the shore of Gunsight Lake: "There, on its haunches, stood a buckskin colored grizzly, as big as a 1,000 pound horse."

According to the 1929 newspaper article:

He showed no fear and apparently had no inclination to fight. The three stood regarding each other for a few moments but when a small group of tourists came up laughing and talking from the lake shore, the grizzly apparently concluded he was being surrounded. He looked back where the noise was coming from and his soft yellow eyes began to flash angrily and the bristly mane along the back of his neck stood straight. The guides moved into the brush and the grizzly got watchfully down on all fours and meandered off slowly and independently until he was lost to view in the timber.

A few months later, in the fall of 1915, after the tourist season was over and Gunsight Chalet had been boarded up for the winter, the Giant Grizzly reportedly attacked the cabin, supposedly smashing in the door with a single swing of its huge paws and cleanly breaking the cast-iron fasteners. Once inside, his first target may have been a large ham hanging from the ceiling, or perhaps it was a partially filled syrup pail. Whatever happened next is left to conjecture, but the bear wasn't too happy to discover a one-pound can of red pepper. When the mule packer and his crew arrived next June, they found the pepper across the floor, "tables upside down, stove parts all over the building, and every dish taken out of the cupboard and thoroughly broken."

Park authorities knew it was time to deal with the destructive creature. According to the 1929 article, bear hunter Bill Burns was called in to kill the grizzly in the fall of 1916. Armed with his pair of trained bear dogs and a gunnysack of decaying fish parts, Burns dragged the bait around the small meadow within sight of the chalet's porch. The dogs waited on leashes. That night, as a full moon illuminated the mountain meadow, the dogs began to growl softly at an approaching menace. Then a dark, indistinct shape moved out from the willow bushes and scrub spruce. The huge bruin came into full view, eagerly attacking the sack of fish.

The article tells the rest of the story: "The bulldog broke loose and tore at the bear, which hurled him high in the air with one tremendous sweep of a paw. Burns could not aim without endangering the dog, so released the Airedale."

Echoes of the dogs' barking rolled from mountain to mountain as the dogs plunged in again and again for a hold on the bear's throat. The battle raged furiously, with the bear boxing and snapping his vicelike jaws. Both dogs were killed, and the "grizzly retreated to some distant and inaccessible part of the mountains and Burns was unable to track him." The bear's ultimate fate has never been determined. Glacier Park visitors should always remember that they are in bear country—and should especially keep a lookout for tracks bigger than a ten-gallon hat.

The Mysterious Disappearance of the Whitehead Brothers

• 1924 •

Thirteen rangers, two famous Indian guides, and seven tried mountaineers were out for more than two weeks. There never has been a search in the National Parks conducted with more vigor and effort.

—F. M. Goodwin, acting secretary of the interior, September 16, 1924

From a base camp at the junction of Mineral and McDonald Creeks, Chauncey "Chance" Beebe, his partner, Jim Whilt, and their pack of four dogs had been searching for Joe and Bill Whitehead for nearly a month. In the early morning of Sunday, August 24, 1924, the two brothers had walked away from Granite Park Chalet and quietly vanished somewhere into the dark depths of forest en route to the Lewis Hotel at Lake McDonald.

Unfortunately, early heavy snowfalls had blanketed the ground before the search team could find anything more than a few unspecified "human artifacts." Considering the efficiency of wilderness scavengers and the approaching winter, it became less and less likely that even the brothers' bones would be discovered. Grudgingly, park officials soon agreed that it was doubtful that the Whitehead brothers were ever going to be found.

The climate, wildlife, and topography of Glacier's back-country, even the established trails such as the brothers were thought to have used, have their share of hazards, especially for the weak or meek. The stark photographs on the reward poster showed twenty-nine-year-old Joseph and twenty-two-year-old William to be a pair of well-dressed, impeccably groomed city boys. Cautious and conservative, they wrote their mother, Dora, every day. In a letter dated August 20, Joe wrote, "We are enjoying ourselves very much and taking no chances of injuring ourselves." Investigators sadly noted the brothers' last words home: "Don't worry, Mother, we won't go into any danger."

By the time they disappeared, the Whiteheads had had over a week's experience tramping around the park. Since arriving at Glacier Park Station on the Great Northern's Oriental Limited on August 17, they had taken excursions to Iceberg Lake, Grinnell Glacier, and Cracker Lake. Eventually they traveled by auto, launch, and horseback from Glacier Park Lodge to Granite Park Chalet and were ready to begin their next adventure. Their 20-mile hike from the chalet to the Lewis Hotel, which is now the Lake McDonald Lodge, would be their most ambitious foray into the park. On August 24 they set off, planning to board the train for home after they returned.

When neither Bill nor Joe stepped off the train to meet their mother on September 1, the search for the boys began. The last credible witnesses to see the two knickers-clad hikers had met them on a trail estimated to be about 10 miles from Lake McDonald's Lewis Hotel, midday on August 24. In addition, three packers for the Park Saddle Horse Company reported seeing the pair near a Logan Creek snowshoe shelter, which was near the upper northwest end of the McDonald Valley. A third sighting came from Jack Jessup of Alberta, Canada, who responded to an inquiry from chief ranger J. P. Brooks: "When Bob Lyford and I was deadheading we met two men on the trail from Grait to Lewis they look like about 20 years of age. We met them about half way to Lewis and that was all the hikers on the trail."

Any imaginative pessimist can conjure up many possible scenarios explaining the boys' disappearance: They might have been hopelessly lost or drowned; they could have fallen down some fathomless glacial crevasse or over some sheer precipice; or perhaps they became a grizzly's lunch. Whatever had happened to the boys, their disappearance kicked off the most extensive search operation ever conducted in a national park. News of the search efforts reached all the way to Washington, D. C., and President Coolidge took interest and wired park officials to spare no expense.

Hope of finding the two brothers was slow to wane among park service personnel. They knew they had an excellent search team out in the wilderness, led by Chance Beebe. Beebe had grown up around the Flathead River's north fork and had been a Glacier ranger from 1917 to 1920. He left the park service to join the Biological Survey (precursor to the present-day U.S. Fish and Wildlife Service) to hunt coyotes, grizzlies, and mountain lions. If anybody knew Glacier's backcountry, it was Chance Beebe. He seemed the man best equipped to find the missing Whitehead brothers, who hadn't been seen since August 24.

On September 16, after fifteen days, Superintendent Kraebel called off search operations. Expenses were rising, rangers needed to get back to their posts because of a high fire danger, and they could think of no other places to check. Interestingly, on the last day of the official effort, a "huge grizzly" was reported to have forced a search party away from the Hidden Lake area. Some suspected this hostile bruin had been the cause of the lads' demise, but this notion wasn't followed up on, according to park archives.

There are two main theories regarding what happened to Bill and Joe. The first suggests that the boys died a natural death, that they fell prey to some kind of natural accident, perhaps a wild-animal attack or a fall; however, a fall seemed unlikely to many investigators, who came to the conclusion that the boys would not have taken chances mountain climbing or embarking on risky explorations. People in the park who met the Whiteheads emphasized their extraordinary efforts to stay safe and reassure their mother. Furthermore, searchers checked every possible creek, cliff, and crevasse without finding a thing. Regarding the frightening possibility of an animal attack, park officials remained skeptical. They held a stubborn confidence that some trace would have been left to indicate this scenario.

A second theory suggests that the Whitehead brothers were victims of foul play, perhaps abduction or murder. This hypothesis rapidly gained credence and eventually became the most widely accepted theory on the fate of the Whitehead brothers, even though there is no evidence to support it. Chance Beebe speculated that they had met someone on the road, several miles from the Lewis Hotel, who caused their disappearance. Even without persuasive evidence of any kind, the authorities pursued this angle with vigor, and Dora Whitehead accepted the possibility quickly, writing to Kraebel on October 21: "My two sons were murdered or kidnapped in a National Park and I am pleading with the Government of the United States to find them."

In November Hubert Work, secretary of the interior, wrote National Park Service acting director, Arno Cammerer, that the grieving mother felt sure her boys "were the victims of a hold-up somewhere on that trail . . . perhaps recruited for work in mines, lumber camps, etc., near the park." Secretary Work requested that the Bureau of Investigation, then headed by J. Edgar Hoover, get involved, and special agent Harold F. Fry from the Butte, Montana, office and agent E. C. Shanahan from the Chicago office were assigned to the case. Shanahan interviewed

Mrs. Whitehead and acquaintances of the brothers while Fry checked out local leads.

Shanahan came up with the same information others already had found: The brothers were cautious and had no known enemies or reason to disappear. Agent Fry reinterviewed the Park Saddle Horse Company packers, certain that the boys they had seen had been the Whiteheads. Fry noted that another horse party that had left the Granite Park Chalet for the Lewis Hotel an hour after the brothers had seen no hikers, although they did report meeting the packers. When considering possible suspects, Fry suggested that the sudden departure from Belton on August 28 of "two notorious characters and alleged bootleggers," R. S. "Dude" Lockett and J. A. "Jack" McDonald, indicated potential outlaws who might have met the boys and harmed them. Follow-up investigations proved fruitless, and neither man was ever taken into custody. Fry wrote in his report that of all the theories advanced, "the most unlikely of those is the bodily abduction [of the brothers] from the Park" and that they could not "pass out unnoticed" against their will.

Of all the bizarre rumors, the strangest came from Eva Beebe, wife of Chance Beebe. She wrote to the Justice Department on March 7, 1933, that "I hold the complete story of the murder." Hoping to secure the reward offered for information about the boys' disappearance, she reported that in October 1925 Jack McDonald, who was one of the men Fry had investigated, and a woman told her they had killed the Whiteheads. Eva went on to relay their claim that they had worked with Dude Lockett to lure the boys to their cabin on Lake Five, just a few miles out of Belton. After a drink-induced violent quarrel, the woman had shot the boys and dumped their weighted bodies into the lake. Eva said that Jack McDonald and this mystery woman had later been caught in Canada for the murder of a taxi driver. McDonald had been executed, and the woman remained in prison.

Butte agent D. H. Dickason investigated "all the possible phases of Mrs. Beebe's story" and concluded that he did "not believe that Mrs. Beebe's story warrants further investigating." And although Mrs. Beebe told the same basic story until her death in 1978, a later private investigation led by park superintendent E. T. Scoyen learned from the Royal Canadian Mounted Police that there was absolutely no record in Canada of the events she described.

So what happened to the Whitehead brothers? No one knows, and without solid evidence, there's nothing left but speculation. Through the decades the Glacier wilderness has remained silent, divulging no clues. It is, as Agent Dickason wrote in 1928, "the most perplexing and inexplicable mystery on our records." The park is a big place. Measured against that, two young men seem very small indeed.

Highway to the Sky
· 1933 ·

There is no road anywhere that is quite like the Sun Road. There are things up there that you just aren't going to find anywhere else.

—Mark Hufstetler, historian

It's a long way down!

—Toni Cook, first-time Going-to-the-Sun visitor

It was 1933, and no one could believe his or her eyes. It didn't seem possible that 5,000 people were milling around at Logan Pass. It certainly didn't seem possible to the local American Indians present. They and their ancestors, traveling through the area for centuries, had always referred to the high mountains now called Glacier National Park as "the backbone of the world," honoring its rugged, high, and impassable nature. Even the national and state politicians who had gathered at the pass, including Montana governor Frank Cooney and U.S. senators Burton Wheeler and W. A. Buchanan, were amazed. They had been influential in securing congressional funding for the construction of the road through Glacier, but discussing it and seeing it were two different matters. But perhaps no one was more pleased or amazed than Duncan McDonald, the pioneer mountain man for whom Lake McDonald was named.

There had been any number of reasons the doubters and naysayers had listed over the years when speaking of the difficulty of building a road across Glacier Park. And yet, it was built.

The Transmountain Highway, which eventually became the amazing Going-to-the-Sun Road, had an unimpressive beginning. The first builders who punched a few miles of ruts from Belton (West Glacier) to Apgar, near Lake McDonald, probably had no idea what they were setting off. It certainly wouldn't have felt to them that they were beginning a road that would climb to 6,646 feet above sea level. After all, they were stuck in the low forests and swampland, spending their days cutting hemlocks and red cedars and dynamiting stumps. William R. Logan, the first superintendent of the park and the man for whom the high pass where the road crests is named, estimated that the crew spent at least $1,000 on dynamite just to blow up the stumps in the first 2½ miles they built. Nevertheless, their start proved that roads could travel up into Glacier's towering mountains. Most people knew that a road penetrating at least some of the west side of the park would be built, but could that same road continue over the Continental Divide?

It could, and it does. From a design and construction standpoint, and also to anyone driving on it, the 52 miles of road called Going-to-the-Sun are a priceless marvel. A trip to Glacier is not complete without a drive along the famous wonder. This invigorating route, sometimes virtually climbing the sides of sheer mountain walls, gained its original "Transmountain Highway" name from mere practical description. Once Congress authorized funding for the road in 1921 to the tune of $100,000, park officials decided they needed a name with a little more zing. But it wasn't until the early 1930s that Montana congressman Louis Cramton proposed "Going-to-the-Sun Road" after a grand eastside mountain near Logan Pass.

The name gained popularity. Superintendent J. R. Eakin became a proponent, liking a name that gave the impression of driving up "to extreme heights" and "sublime panoramas." It also fit with local legend. Among the Blackfeet, tales were told of a benevolent spirit who comes out of the sky to help out in a time of trouble only to ascend back up toward the sun once his task is completed. The traditional Blackfeet name for the mountain is The-Face-of-Sour-Spirit-Who-Went-Back-to-the-Sun-after-His-Work-Was-Done. Unsurprisingly, it was shortened to Going-to-the-Sun.

It took almost twenty years and $3 million to plan and build the road. Crews began work on the road from the west side early in the park's life, but it wasn't until 1921 that a continuous effort was made to build a road across the Continental Divide. At present it can only be imagined what they thought as they looked up at Logan Pass and at their simple hand tools and pondered the amazing construction project before them. And yet, they were successful. The west side of Going-to-the-Sun Road opened in June 1929. Four years later, on July 15, 1933, the east side was completed, and the road was officially dedicated. Of the estimated 5,000 people who attended the dedication ceremony on Logan Pass, two of the important local American Indian tribe members were Kootenai chief Kustata and Blackfeet chief Two-Guns White Calf, as well as Flathead leaders. These former adversaries blessed the road and smoked a peace pipe together to celebrate their modern harmony.

But before anyone could gather to celebrate, work crews had toiled and sweated for years. All workers had to have confidence and daring, for in many places the sheer rock walls didn't have even enough horizontal surface to stand on, and there were great stretches where a path had to be blasted out of solid rock. Dynamite crews were lowered down precipitous cliffs to drill sets of holes into the rock face to house explosives for detonation. In Rose Houk's book *Going-to-the-Sun Road: The Story of the Highway across Glacier Park,* Frank A. Kittredge, a Bureau of Public Roads engineer who led a surveying crew in 1924, reports that it was difficult to keep the crews fully staffed. "The daily climb of from 1,200' to 3,000' over cliffs and through brush proved too strenuous for many. Work on the line along the steep mountainside and cliffs proved too hazardous for those not adapted to such work. Working in the rain and sleet was beyond endurance for many more."

Despite the high dropout rate, the road did slowly emerge. Kittredge's surveying crew recommended a route over Logan Pass because of its south and west exposures. This meant, of course, that the road would be in sunlight and not under the shadows of the surrounding peaks as much as possible. In an area where snowfalls are extremely deep, this was an important consideration.

In the late 1920s six campsites were set up on the west side of the pass, where the workmen, many of whom were World War I veterans, lived and ate. Teams of horses worked a system of travois and sleds to supply the workers and transport equipment. Pneumatic hammers powered by heavy compressors were used to attack the rock, while limited-track gas locomotives lugged out tons of excavated debris. Some of the first Ford dump trucks also joined in the effort.

The men's wages, quite decent for the times, may have helped to improve the moods of the brave but uncomfortable workers: The pay for excavation work was approximately $1.15 an hour, although less-skilled laborers earned more like 50 cents per hour. By present-day standards this hardly seems imaginable, especially given the kinds of peril the workmen faced. The obstacles must have seemed endless. The possibility of a deadly slip was constant. Steep slopes were prone to rockfalls and debris slides. In order to protect themselves, some workers wore World War I infantry helmets as some of the world's first "hard hats." However, there were not enough of these to go around, so many workers simply wore their felt hats and derbies. Another source of worry for the workmen was the hungry bears that loitered around their camps. As always, necessity was the mother of invention: The men adapted to the bears by hanging their lunches from saws suspended in tree branches.

A final obstacle was the weather. The short summer season in Glacier meant construction lasted for an intense three or four months at a time, which is the primary reason that the job took more than a decade by calendar but only around a year and a half of work days. Winter conditions sometimes undid work that had been completed the previous summer, and parts of the road had to be rebuilt each spring. Just the massive amount of snowfall was a problem, as workers had to clear giant drifts before they could get to work again.

Yet despite all these barriers, the road was built with only three tragedies. A failed rope dropped Charles Rudberg to the roadbed in 1926. Five years later a falling rock struck and killed Carl Rosenquist. In 1932, the same year the road was completed, Gus Swanson was caught in a rockslide.

Going-to-the-Sun Road proved vital to Glacier tourism. Although it was completed during the Great Depression, the new attraction brought 43 percent more visitation than the park had seen in the year before its opening. Park officials estimate that about 40,000 people drove over the Sun Road during its first year—ten times the total visitation in 1911. Now the road sees upward of two million annual visitors in more than 500,000 vehicles.

The heavy visitation has taken its toll on the road, but the harsh weather conditions and alpine environment cause many problems as well. The famous "Loop," a tight, nearly 180-degree turn on the west side, was constructed with stacked stone blocks, which are now slumping out from the slope. Constant movement called "ground creep" shifts and warps the road's foundation, even along flat areas. Frequent avalanches and rockslides during the winter months also cause damage, and age alone has caused cracks and the need for patches in the pavement. Going-to-the-Sun Road is indeed in need of repair. Renovation work has been going on for a few years, but major solutions are still being determined, as an all-out construction closure would seriously slow tourism and damage local businesses. Added into this complex mix is the fact that Sun Road is on the National Register of Historic Places as a National Civil Engineering Landmark, necessitating careful construction parameters to maintain its historic integrity.

Driving over Going-to-the-Sun Road is a marvelous experience—and occasionally a dangerous one. Even in the height of a dry summer, rockfalls are common. In 1996 a gigantic boulder broke off the Garden Wall and crushed a Japanese tourist who had the extreme misfortune to be driving below at the time. On another occasion a falling boulder smashed down onto a popular local newspaperman's car, flattening the back half of his vehicle. Though the newspaperman escaped uninjured, his wife still suffers lingering difficulties as a result of the accident. Over the years road crews have been buried by avalanches, and equipment has fallen over the edge. Intrepid hikers below Bird Woman Walls can still find the remains of a twisted front-end loader that took a dive years ago. Perhaps present-day visitors would be wise to follow the cautionary advice given to Glacier's visitors in 1924: "Automobiles in motion must be not less than fifty yards apart, except when passing. Speed is 12 miles on grades, 20 miles on open stretches."

The Great Fire

· 1936 ·

From the scenic standpoint this is a major
disaster of first magnitude.

—E. T. Scoyen, Glacier Park superintendent,
August 31, 1936

Glacier Park superintendent E. T. Scoyen knew more than
he cared to about what fires could do in Glacier National Park.
In his first year at the park, in the mid-1920s, brush-burning operations caused a large fire at St. Mary, even though there were
several snowbanks around, which had been expected to keep
matters under control. Then, a devastating 1929 conflagration
had destroyed nearly 100,000 Montana acres—47,000 acres in
the park—when it swept in from the west side. Furthermore, in
October 1934, some late-season brush fires got out of control.
Up until September 30 of that year, Scoyen and his staff had
managed to keep the season's fire losses to less than one hundred acres. Quite pleased by this, he didn't want to take any
chances and was therefore waiting until an 18-inch snowfall
blanketed the Many Glacier region before calling out the Civil-
ian Conservation Corp (CCC) to dispose of accumulated brush
piles by removing or burning them. Nevertheless, before the
snows fell and the brush could be disposed of by human
hands, nature took over. On October 4, 1934, a fire broke out
and threatened to destroy the entire area around Sherburne
Lake near Many Glacier. As it burned through the evening, the

Swiftcurrent Valley was illuminated much as it would have been in the middle of the day. Luckily, this late-season fire didn't turn into a major disaster.

Based on these experiences Scoyen came to the conclusion that the only safe time to burn brush was the middle of winter. If the fire danger was so extreme even with a dusting of snow on the ground, imagine what could happen during the summer months. Superintendent Scoyen was about to find out.

On August 18, 1936, lightning struck the steep southeast side of Heaven's Peak, a massive mountain on the west side of the park. Located in rugged terrain nearly impossible for humans to reach, the fire smoldered for several days. On August 21 the growing blaze became visible from Going-to-the-Sun Road. Still, the smoldering fire's potential was underestimated. Robert W. Virtue, a tourist from New Orleans, later wrote a chastising letter to the National Park Service with his assessment:

> While passing through Glacier National Park a few weeks ago, I reported a small fire to a ranger. He thanked me and replied that it had been burning a week but was "under control." That was the McDonald Creek Fire. A very small amount of chemicals could have put that fire OUT. I'm sure that one whole day's work by one person could have put the fire out when I saw it, for not more than six trees were burning. (I had glasses available, so could see it at fairly close range).

Scoyen's reply to Virtue's letter stated that the fire

> was burning in a very deep blanket of pine needles and duff [decaying organic matter on the forest floor] and was . . . on the face of a cliff which is a great deal steeper than it appears from the highway. There was absolutely no dirt or water available to smother

the fire and to date no chemical has been devised which will control a duff fire burning in the open. The only thing we were able to do was to trench each of the fires that we could reach. Some of the smaller spots . . . we were not able to get men on at all, although in places we were letting men down over the cliff at the end of five hundred feet of rope.

Despite these efforts the smoldering fire on Heaven's Peak broke into open burning on August 21, and men were immediately dispatched to the site. Scoyen had not exaggerated the steepness of the terrain, and firefighters were forced to climb to the top of an area of the mountain known locally as the Glacial Wall, an enormous rocky face that had born the brunt of glacial erosion eons ago. Initially, they managed to stop the fire after it had spread twenty acres; however, the fire eventually broke over the edge of the cliffs, sending flaming embers down into innumerable crevices packed with dry moss, lichen, and debris. Unbelievably, heat from the fire caused rocks and boulders, some weighing many tons, to break loose and plummet thousands of feet to the valley below, endangering the firefighters in the area. Even when these men were able to reach burning sites, they found the fires difficult to put out due to the lack of extinguishing materials such as mineral soil and water.

For nearly a week crews battled to contain the fire to the cliffs. Scoyen reported in a telegram to National Park Service director Cammerer in Washington, D.C., on August 22: "Lightning fire on McDonald Creek may do serious damage to scenic features along Logan Pass Highway if winds blow up today. Have three hundred men on line and hope for some luck."

By the next day it seemed that some good luck had come. Scoyen optimistically reported: "We have controlled 12 fires started in park past 24 hours by lightning and a total of 23 since Friday. McDonald Creek under control with practically no scenic or other damage. Two very large fires burning on Flathead

Forest opposite north of Logging and Quartz creeks giving us great concern and we have sent in 200 men to supplement the 1,000 Forest Service on the line."

Two days later, on August 25, things looked even better: "Light rains greatly improved fire situation and everything out with practically no damage."

Unfortunately, on August 30, high winds blew the fire across containment lines. The flames swept into thickly timbered areas and immediately blazed out of control. Nonetheless, with five hundred CCC and other park personnel on the line, Scoyen expected to regain control by the next day. His first telegram of the day reported that the fire was spreading rapidly but that control was still within reach. A second telegram, barely two hours later, warned that the fire had now crossed Going-to-the-Sun Road, necessitating immediate, indefinite closure. He planned to have 700 men on the line later that morning.

The winds continued into the next day, overcoming the efforts of the firefighters and roaring up the mountains toward and past the Granite Park Chalet, which had been evacuated. Scoyen's telegram that afternoon was short and terse: "High winds blew all fires completely out of control this afternoon . . . have ample organization [to] handle situation if conditions get back to normal." But normal conditions were not to be: Driven by the wind, the blazing fire raced over 8,000-foot-high Swiftcurrent Pass, heading straight for Many Glacier Valley and a tinder-dry lodge.

Suddenly, saving the lodge became the focus of attention, and all available hands were required to try to make it happen. John Turner was spending his first summer in the park as a jammer (short for "gear jammer," a driver of one of the park's trademark red open-air buses), relaxing on his day off at East Glacier when Sid Couch, the Many Glacier jammer dispatcher, put in an urgent call for all buses to be sent as soon as possible to evacuate the guests at the threatened lodge. Turner and another bus driver headed out immediately, their engine governors limiting them to a 40-mile-per-hour crawl. By the time they arrived in Many Glacier from East Glacier, it was late afternoon; the fire had already jumped over the Garden Wall above Grinnell Glacier and was heading for the lodge. "The intensity of the heat was generating a virtual firestorm," Turner related, "and the resulting wind was gaining force as it pushed the fire down the valley toward Many Glacier." Most of the hundred hotel guests had already been evacuated when Turner arrived, but some decided to stay behind and become impromptu firefighters in an attempt to save the historic hotel.

According to Turner, "The entire Swiftcurrent Valley, along with Grinnell Mountain and Mount Altyn, were ablaze. The wind was so intense across the lake it was literally picking up sheets of water and misting the hotel structure. Some of us were convinced that this strange phenomenon played a significant part in helping the firefighters save the hotel from burning down." The gear jammers, under the direction of Sid Couch, fought the spot fires that were breaking out all around the employee dormitories, the gear-jammer dorm, and the transport garage. "The air was filled with red burning debris, cinders and smoke, igniting one fire after another and making breathing a significant problem," said Turner. "Covering our heads with wet rags helped somewhat. Strong wind gusts made it very difficult to move around and keep balanced."

By late that evening the winds had subsided, and thanks to the Herculean efforts of soot-covered firefighters, rangers, jammers, hotel staff, and bold guests—and the fact that the hotel had a slate roof—Many Glacier Lodge was saved. Eventually, the fire was brought under control by a merciful rain that fell late that night.

The total scorched area amounted to 7,642 acres of timber, grassland, and subalpine fir. A few game animals were killed along with major populations of fish in Swiftcurrent Creek. Amazingly, there were no human casualties. Damages were estimated at $25,000. The fire destroyed the Many Glacier chalet complex, about ninety cabins, an auto tourist camp, a ranger station, an icehouse, a saddle-horse corral, and several other small structures.

A record sixty-seven fires plagued Glacier in 1936 due to an abnormally hot May—when much of the snow cover melted earlier in the season than normal—and very low precipitation levels in July and August. The origins of these sixty-seven fires were reported to be as follows: one caused by campers, one caused by incinerator sparks, one caused by a wrecked automobile, twenty-six caused by careless smokers, and thirty-eight caused by lightning. The three that reached Class C (greater than ten acres) were lightning-caused, but only the Heaven's Peak blaze grew to major proportions. The busiest period for the firefighters was from August 21 to August 23, when a total of fourteen fires erupted at widely separated sites. Glacial recession surveys in 1936 also reflected the hot summer's effect on the park's glaciers, recording a recession rate fully eight times the average for the previous four years.

The 1936 Heaven's Peak Fire remains one of the park's most devastating events. Effects can still be clearly seen today as a grim reminder—and clear warning—to all.

Survival Story

· 1953 ·

It is almost a case of tradition that all of the park is
open to visitors by June 15.

—Jack W. Emmert,
former Glacier Park superintendent

Winter's annual grip on Glacier National Park is long and
strong. Consequently, the opening of Going-to-the-Sun Road
each year is accomplished by hardy road crews whose battles
are fought with great snow-removal machines and ever-present
danger. Their courage, hard work, and tenacity allows tourists
the privilege of traveling that grand highway in the sky. Amid
monstrous snowpacks up to 70 feet deep and the constant
threat of avalanches, these crews must perform backbreaking
work mere feet from cliff edges. It's amazing that the task can
be accomplished at all, much less annually.

Perhaps equally amazing is that only a single tragedy has
struck the road-clearing crews in Going-to-the-Sun's more than
fifty-year existence. And even that disaster is illuminated with
the glowing flame of human triumph.

In May 1953 road-clearing efforts began just as they had
in previous years, despite cool spring temperatures. The road
on the west side of the park was open all the way to the tight
hairpin curve known as the Loop, with similar progress reaching toward Logan Pass on the east. Drifts were attacked with
bulldozers, which cut into the snow again and again until ro-

tary plows could come through to slough off the remaining few feet of snow on the roadway—slow progress, but progress nonetheless.

Then on May 21 the beginnings of a fierce spring storm moved in. Initially, the storm just refreshed the valleys with a light rain while blanketing the higher elevations with wet snow. By May 24, however, the weather system had developed into a full-blown blizzard, dumping nearly 2 feet of new, sloppy snow on the Continental Divide.

A park report stated:

> Snow-removal operations have been retarded because the crews repeatedly are required to retrace their operations and remove either fresh snow or snow that covered the highway from small slides. Because of these unusual conditions, supervisory personnel have issued definite instructions that all the men in the snow-removal crews must not work in any location that appeared to be exceptionally dangerous.

It is doubtful this type of warning would have persuaded any of the road-crew foremen to stay inside by the fire. Each one of the foremen had nearly two decades of experience and was well aware of the danger that always accompanied his task. Each one approached his job with respect for the mountains and a positive, can-do attitude.

When the storm began to clear on the morning of Tuesday, May 26, mixed-gang foreman Ray Price decided to leave his Garden Wall camp to check out the damage, and he wasn't surprised by what he found. The heavy wet snow, falling on older snow made slick by rain and ice, had triggered several small avalanches of snow, rock, and trees. Slides had also thundered down the usual avalanche corridors below the Triple Arches, the Weeping Wall, and the Haystack Creek funnel.

Price assigned a crew to reclear this area and then went on to his own work a couple miles above.

By 8:30 that morning crew members Fred Klein and Bill Whitford had begun the assault on the Haystack Creek slide— a 105-foot long, 15-foot-deep mass of snow. No bulldozer was available to them, and the heavy wet snow meant slow progress for their Snogo (a light rotary plow). When road supervisor M. E. "Jean" Sullivan arrived in his pickup with mixed-gang foreman George "Blackie" Beaton to survey the situation at 10:30 that morning, Sullivan decided they would make better progress if they blasted the snowpack with dynamite. He unloaded fifty pounds of dynamite, then took over Klein's position on the compacted snow beside the recent Snogo cut and continued scouting for avalanches while Klein went back to the pickup for the detonator caps. Foreman George Beaton assumed his own watchman stance on the Snogo's hood; Bill Whitford waited in the cab.

"I had asked Bill, who had his head stuck out of the cab window, and George if they thought using the dynamite was safe," Sullivan recalled later. "George said, 'Hell, yes, Jean. Let's blow it out and we'll be outta here in 30 minutes.' He just got the words out of his mouth when I heard a little swish. We call this slide a 'sneaker.' I looked up and the snow slide was coming—no more than 80 feet above us—and I hollered."

The avalanche started on a side slope, out of anyone's sight, then slammed into the Haystack Creek funnel and down on the men. It roared across the roadway, wider even than the original slide the men had come to clean up, sweeping men and machinery alike over the side of the road in a storm of flying snow, rock, and debris.

According to Sullivan, "I jumped into the hole that the Snogo had cut out, to keep myself from going down over the bank. When I jumped, George [Beaton] was not over six or eight feet from me, and I saw him between the Snogo and the outside edge of the road. When the slide hit the Snogo, I was not covered yet, and I heard the impact and saw the Snogo going over. It sounded like barrels of bottles being rattled. I know that Beaton was between it and the outside edge of the road, and Whitford was in the cab. There was snow in the air. Bill Whitford didn't have a chance."

Sullivan recalled his thoughts before he lost consciousness: "I was covered. I worked my head back and forth, and my hands a little. The snow was heavy. I thought of [my wife] May, but I wasn't cold or afraid for myself. I knew they would dig me out. I was worried about what happened to Whitford and Beaton, and I didn't know about Freddie [Klein]. It became hard to breathe. I kept breathing faster and faster and apparently passed out."

Not a single sign remained of men or machinery. The new avalanche had completely covered up all trace of the men's previous efforts, except for Sullivan's lonely pickup at the slide's edge.

No other crews heard or saw the avalanche. At noon Foreman Price decided to walk down the 2 miles from his work along the Weeping Wall to find out what had halted the lower operations. What he saw at Haystack was puzzling. Price knew this slide was supposed to have been worked on, but the fresh snow made it look totally untouched. There was no sign of men or the Snogo, just an empty pickup.

"I decided that the other plow must have broken down," Price said, "and that they took it back to the Garden Wall road camp to work on it. So I started walking down the road to the camp." Before getting there he met up with the afternoon relief crew, dutifully hiking up to relieve the morning guys, whose shift was supposed to end at one o'clock. No one had seen or passed men or plow. Price immediately realized what had happened and raced down to the camp to alert park headquarters.

After securing a vehicle, Price drove with the four relief crew members up to the avalanche site, splitting them into two-man search teams. Within minutes they'd found Fred Klein, 300 feet below the roadway. He was alive but badly injured. Just ten minutes later, another 300 feet below Klein, they found Bill Whitford, thrown clear from the Snogo's cab and completely buried except for a boot tip. He was dead, having suffered a broken neck and chest injuries. The searchers frantically resumed their efforts.

A twelve-man gravel road crew from Logan Creek arrived, equipped with probes, shovels, first-aid equipment, and front-end loaders. The rescue force continued to swell: Within two hours they were joined by park employees, Great Northern railway crews, private construction gangs from a Highway 2 project, state highway workers from a Coram bridge project, and even Sullivan and Beaton's West Glacier neighbors.

Park supervisors based their rescue efforts on the theory that Sullivan and Beaton were buried in the thinner snow on the road's outer edges. Some volunteers disagreed, among them a park-service roadman, Dimon Apgar, a descendant of the man who had established Apgar Village near Lake McDonald at the turn of the century and Sullivan's close friend.

Apgar heeded his instincts and tried to recreate the scene in his mind. From a slight hump of snow on the road's inward side, he correctly guessed that the Snogo had begun its trench and that a man, seeking protection, might have leaped into the trench. For the next few hours, while others probed the outside edges, Apgar dug his bar into the hump's overhang. After about a dozen such probes, he uncovered Sullivan's head. Jean was alive! It took until seven o'clock to finally free his body. Sullivan was immediately dispatched to a Kalispell hospital, and with renewed hope, the searchers continued their efforts to find Beaton.

In the predawn hours the next morning, Flathead County sheriff Dick Walsh arrived with George Talbott and Talbott's bloodhound, Joy. Beginning at 6:00 A.M., the bloodhound scoured the avalanche site and finally located Beaton under 3 feet of snow, 1,200 feet below the highway. From the extent of his injuries, the rescuers concluded that Beaton had probably died instantly.

Fred Klein, the first man to be found, never fully recovered, and he quickly retired on a disability pension. Bill Whitford and George Beaton's lives were honored by their families, many friends, and by park employees. Joy, the bloodhound, received a badge as an honorary park ranger. And Jean Sullivan? Despite being buried for more than seven hours, he was out of the hospital in only three days—and back to snow-clearing operations within a few weeks. He eventually retired from the park service and lived comfortably with his wife until his death in 1972.

Due to continued bad weather and deep snowpack, Going-to-the-Sun Road didn't open that year until June 24, the latest opening date on record. So, the next time you drive along one of the most spectacular roads in America, knuckles white as you grip the steering wheel, remind yourself that you have the easy job. And salute those courageous crews who clear the roads each and every spring.

The Great Flood of 1964

· 1964 ·

The floods of June, 1964 are the Glacier country's greatest disaster since the extermination of the buffalo.

—Edmund Christianson,
in *Adventure among the Glaciers*

The spring of 1964 was long and cold—hardly atypical for northwestern Montana, where blue skies and warm temperatures are sometimes hard to come by, a place where summer is like an old but faithful engine that starts up only after a frustrating session of cranking. In 1964 spring seemed to have an especially hard time maturing into summer. The previous winter had seen an above-average snowfall, so the high country still had substantially large snowbanks. Slowly but surely, these snowbanks were melting and filling the park's streambeds and low places with water. This replenishment process follows an ancient rhythm; however, this year, the runoff levels were unusually high.

On Sunday, June 7, it began to rain. And rain. And then it rained some more. After a two-day drenching, Glacier Park headquarters at West Glacier measured a staggering 4.62 inches of rainfall. Browning, a town on the Blackfeet reservation on the opposite side of the park, normally received about 15 inches annually, but within those forty-eight hours, this small town received a soaking 8 inches, more than half its average yearly total! Some people estimate that the rainfall totals in the high country were an amazing 12 inches.

In the days following the deluge, the weather began to warm, causing the snowpack to melt rapidly. The runoff from the melting snow, combined with the rainwater already gushing through the park, virtually assured catastrophe. The immediate effects of the flooding were dramatic and deadly: Gentle mountain streams became raging torrents; dry gulches became rivers; roads became impassable; and travel became a lesson in danger.

At the lodge at Lake McDonald, the losses were devastating. Don Hummel, the head of Glacier Park, Inc., at the time, described the destruction in Ray Djuff and Chris Morrison's book *View with a Room—Glacier's Historic Hotels & Chalets:*

> Snyder Creek had rampaged down the mountain undermining huge cedar trees which formed a dam that diverted the flood directly into the hotel. The dining room had been undermined, an empty shell hanging over eroded stream banks. Its floor lay at the bottom of the creek. The big stone fireplace that had stood at its far end was completely gone. Ragged logs and the tattered remains of its roof hung over empty space.

Kitchen staff were forced to work in a makeshift kitchen and dining room. The destruction was particularly disappointing to Donald Knutson, the hotel manager since 1957, who had recently overseen a total lobby renovation, the modernization of the kitchen and dining room, and the addition of bath facilities in ten rooms. The flood undid much of the work.

Hummel sat in his office, organizing disaster efforts and waiting for reports from across the park. The news wasn't good:

- In the Swiftcurrent Valley the only road to Many Glacier was hopelessly washed out, cutting off Many Glacier Lodge from the outside world for a full eight days. First-floor rooms looking out at Swiftcurrent Lake literally lived up to their description as "Lake Level Rooms" when flood-waters sloshed in to a height of 3 feet.
- St. Mary Lake spilled out and flooded its namesake town.
- West Glacier Bridge was twisted, its roadbed fractured and tilted, and the whole structure threatened to crash into the tumultuous Middle Fork Flathead River. Downstream, a record 26-foot-high crest surged down the river near the town of Columbia Falls. The gushing waters actually reversed the flow of McDonald Creek, turning the water-course from an outlet to an inlet and raising the level of Lake McDonald 8 feet over the high-water mark.
- At the southern end of the park, large portions of U.S. Highway 2 were washed out, turning hundred-yard sections into miniwaterfalls as the runoff gushed over the road and plummeted down to the Flathead River. The Walton Bridge on that highway eventually succumbed to the water as well.
- On the east side of the park, superintendent William Grissom worked heroically with Blackfeet Agency staff to warn locals and perform dozens of rescues. American Indian ranchers who depended on Two Medicine Dam for irrigation were horrified to witness its collapse. The sudden flood of water caught up and swept away seventeen people attempting to escape in a pickup truck, only nine of whom survived. Malmstrom Air Force Base helicopters were called in to rescue other stranded citizens.
- At Birch Creek in the Heart Butte region, the 157-foot-tall Swift Dam gave way, drowning twenty-five Blackfeet. Washouts and bridge damage left sections of the Great Northern Railroad tracks hanging precariously.

While most observers saw only disaster and destruction, and perhaps a ruined tourist season, Hummel saw opportunity. He decided to use the flood as a catalyst to begin long-awaited renovations at the lodges and other concession structures. Many of the lodging and dining facilities were sorely in need of repair even before the disastrous fingers of the flood did their damage. Because the havoc in the park was sure to slow tourism for the foreseeable future, Hummel decided to use the time to bring badly needed upgrades and modernizations to park facilities.

Though the great lodge at East Glacier survived the rising waters untouched, a flood of a different kind had to be contended with—a deluge of hundreds of students arriving for their summer jobs. Hummel turned Glacier Park Hotel into disaster headquarters. In an unusual move the staff moved into the lodge's guest rooms since Hummel assumed that most who were scheduled to arrive any day probably would not.

According to *View with a Room,* Hummel gathered together all employees every night to give them the latest information. "On the third evening I had bad news," Hummel later remarked. "I would be unable to pay anyone until we could get the facilities open and establish a cash flow. I promised everyone room and board without charge. I offered all an opportunity to leave without any reflection on their employment records. Not a single employee left." Hummel describes that as an unmatched moment of pride in his long career. As a result of the hard work by Hummel and all the park employees, the summer tourist season was salvaged. Even the lodge at Lake McDonald, where the the dining room had been destroyed, managed to open for business that summer.

Opening the park that summer proved a daunting task. Going-to-the Sun Road suffered $2.25 million worth of damage and didn't open until June 20. US 2 was reopened on June 9 but only through the use of a "Bailey Bridge"—a portable, pre-fabricated bridge made up of steel lattices, named after its English inventor, Sir D. C. Bailey. It took railroad crews several weeks to restore the Great Northern line, with the first traffic finally moving along the repaired rails on June 29. Though similar circumstances have resulted in other floods in and around Glacier Park, the damage has never come close to what was seen that one soggy June in 1964.

U.S. Air Force Attacks Logan Pass
· 1964 ·

What's your bet going to be this year, Jim?"

"The first of June!" replied Jim, always an optimist. This response evoked a volley of chuckles from the men grouped in twos and threes throughout the cafe. The talk, as usual, had turned to the opening of the Going-to-the-Sun Road. It was the middle of May, and the assembled restaurateurs, hoteliers, mechanics, grocers, and others were itching for the short but sweet busy season to begin.

Clearing snow from Going-to-the-Sun Road has been a major concern for as long as the road has existed. At lower elevations the challenge is simply one of depth and drift: Send in men and machine, and it's a basic equation of mechanics and man-hours. Given sufficient equipment and labor, the asphalt of the lower roads can be uncovered in a matter of days. In the high country, where Going-to-the-Sun earns its name, those same operations must be attempted along sheer cliffs and through massive, eons-old avalanche chutes. Some years, just *locating* the road under 45 or 50 feet of snow is a grand achievement.

But for the businesspeople sipping their coffee in West Glacier that May morning, and for hundreds others just like them from Kalispell to Browning and beyond, clearing the road was neither an epic tale of man versus snow nor a matter of convenience for tourists wanting to see the splendor of Glacier; it was a matter of economics. The road's opening was arguably the most anticipated event of the year. The sooner people could travel through the park, the sooner tourist dollars would start to flow. Anything that could be done to speed the process would get their vote.

Throughout the 1950s substantial time, labor, money, and new equipment were dedicated to snow-clearing operations. All the latest techniques were employed to get the job done; moreover, the park service keenly wanted to minimize the risk factors, the foremost of which was the accidental triggering of overhanging slide areas before they came down on their own. Dynamite charges and even artillery fire were purposely used with only marginal results, and park officials were always searching for ways to knock loose those lurking sheets of snow without actually touching them.

Why not try attacking them from above? In the early 1960s an ex–U.S. Air Force pilot working in the park came up with a novel idea: Use sonic booms to shake the slides loose. Thus was born Project Safe Slide, possibly one of the most unusual missions ever undertaken by the air force.

The idea was as simple as it was dramatic: Send a pair of jet fighters screaming in low over Logan Pass and let the thundering sonic booms send the slides tumbling down the mountain. Remarkably, the bold plan was not dismissed out of hand by park officials, and Project Safe Slide was eventually approved by both the park service and the U.S. Air Force. Pilots from the Twenty-ninth Fighter Interceptor Squadron from Great Falls's Malmstrom Air Force Base were selected for the honor of being the world's first "avalanche shooters." The pilots, Captains William Marshburn and Donald Scully, didn't hesitate one bit in accepting the honor, eager for the unusual opportunity despite the fact that it meant flying low between Glacier's jagged peaks.

The radar observers, Captain David Sommers and Lieutenant Bob Harrison, and operations officer and acting commander Major Cecil C. Foster, signed on enthusiastically as well.

Initial plans took shape in January 1964. Acting park supervisor Jack Dodd scheduled the mission for Monday, March 23. Park engineer Max Edgar, project information officer Lieutenant Clark Duffey, and an air force film crew traveled by car and SnoCat to an observation point.

Having used dynamite to attempt to trigger premature slides in Glacier several times before, without much success, Edgar was doubtful at best. Blizzard conditions on March 21 and 22 made him even more so. March 23 dawned as the coldest day of the season. By the time Edgar and the film crew were positioned, the temperature was a crisp six degrees below zero with a gusty wind blowing. Airborne snow hazed the air, placing the pilots in potentially serious danger.

Nevertheless, after all the time and effort that had been invested, the decision was made to go ahead with the flights. The pilots concluded there was enough visibility to fly down between the rocky peaks, and Information Officer Duffey conceded that even if this attempt was unsuccessful, it would provide valuable information for any later attempts.

At 2:40 in the afternoon, Captain Marshburn followed his lead pilot, Captain Scully, over Logan Pass on an initial practice run in their F-101 Voodoo fighter jets. Minutes later they returned, their jets screaming over the pass at more than 900 miles per hour (15 miles a second)! As Duffey reported, "Because of a combination of factors the shockwaves following the two booms of manmade thunder were spotted racing across the sky to a mountain only slightly over a mile away on the group's right."

"Avalanche!" Edgar yelled, startling the air force film crew. Prior doubts of being able to send off a slide, or having enough contrast to see white snow moving down over a white background, were erased as four mammoth avalanches erupted down the dark rock of Mount Cannon. Cameras whirred, and people gasped.

The Voodoos arced in for a closer and more daring approach. There was no doubt the pilots were enjoying their work. According to Duffey, "At least six more slides let loose, starting in slow motion and gaining speed like freight trains."

If the grizzlies and other hibernating wildlife had not yet awakened from their winter slumber, March 23 was likely their wake-up call. Of course, those people at the site were amazed and awed to see avalanches pounding down the sharp mountain slopes in response to the split-second passes of low-flying aircraft, followed by earsplitting impact. No one knows what local residents and others, uninformed of the plan, not to mention Glacier's wildlife, so used to silence, must have thought of the unusual sounds echoing down the valleys in all directions. No one had ever seen or heard anything like this coming from Glacier before.

A total of eleven sonic-boom-triggered slides were recorded by the ground observers, though in all probability there were several others, hidden from view, that went unrecorded. Project Safe Slide was considered a "startlingly successful break-through from the series of previous failures in the effort to prematurely release slides."

Subsequent efforts that year weren't as successful, as reported in the June 1964 Operations and Training Report of the Twenty-ninth Fighter Interceptor Squadron: "Two 29th F101 aircraft were again used and two supersonic passes were made at altitudes well below the level of the surrounding peaks in an attempt to shake loose some dangerous snowslide areas. Results were not quite as effective as the previous attempt since rough turbulence hampered reaching the 900 MPH speeds that were attained the first time."

Project Safe Slide was eventually abandoned. Only a few pilots got the boasting rights of telling their grandkids that they once traveled over Logan Pass at almost 1,000 miles per hour.

From the beginning critics called the spring road clearing foolish, a vast waste of resources and manpower. But waiting for a natural snowmelt was out of the question, economically speaking. The economic value of the much-publicized "Sun Road" became crystal clear after the road was completed. For example, in 1946, Glacier visitation was tallied at 200,000 people. By 1954, a mere eight years later, that number had tripled to 600,000. Based on information collected in 1951, the average visitor stayed two days in the park and spent $5.00 per day. Without the Going-to-the-Sun Road, at least $1 million dollars per year might not have flowed into the park in the 1950s. And without a little help getting the road cleared, whether from the sky or the ground, those business owners in West Glacier and across the region would have been sitting in their cafes drinking coffee for nine out of twelve months each year.

The Unthinkable
Happens
· 1967 ·

To share a mountain with [the grizzly] for awhile is
a privilege and an adventure like no other.

—Andy Russell, conservationist and grizzly
authority, in *Night of the Grizzlies* by Jack Olsen

What are you saying? Are you sure?" Leonard Landa, a
ranger based out of the Lake McDonald station, was trying to
sort out the story that was spilling from the mouths of a frantic
and disheveled quartet of young people. He had seen them the
day before and knew they were planning to camp at Trout
Lake, but they were now talking about a bear that had attacked
one of the young women in their group.

"Are you saying someone was attacked by a bear?"

"Yes!"

"But I thought you were going to camp at Trout Lake? Do
you mean you went to Granite Park Chalet instead?"

"No! Trout Lake! And Michele is still up there. She's got to
be dead."

Landa had been on the radio all night, helping coordinate
rescue activities at the Granite Park Chalet. Tragically, a young
woman had been fatally wounded by a bear there. Landa's
bleary mind was having trouble piecing together what this

group of young campers was saying, but the sickness in the pit of his stomach grew, since visitors had been complaining all summer of a bear at Trout Lake, rummaging for food and frightening hikers and campers. Still, could it be true that the first and second killings by bears in Glacier Park had happened on the same night?

It could be, and it was. Of course, there had been bear trouble in the past, but it was not frequent and not fatal. For the first thirty years of the park's existence, only one bear attack was reported, and seventeen years passed until the next attack. Over the next decade, the pace picked up with nine attacks reported, but even so, that averaged out to only one attack every five years for the park's first fifty-seven years of operation.

Landa pieced together the story of what had happened. The day before, Saturday, August 12, the five teenagers and their dog had left Lake McDonald and huffed their way up and over a ridge and down to Trout Lake. All five were employed in the park, and all five were looking forward to beating the baking heat of mid-August at a cold mountain lake, passing their time fishing. When they reached Trout Lake, the group split up, with four going to fish while one, Michele Koons, stayed behind to finish setting up camp. Michele was from San Diego and was working that summer at the Lake McDonald Lodge. Before long the four who had been fishing returned, and dinner preparations began. According to Jack Olsen's accounts in *Sports Illustrated* and his book, *Night of the Grizzlies,* Michele was relaxing when she looked toward the woods and saw a shape not 10 feet away. "Here comes a bear!" All five campers ran about 50 yards and noticed that the bear wasn't following them but rather enjoying all the food they had left at camp. It was an ugly-looking bear, mangy and skinny, and if it had been human, they might have described it as acting erratically. It left once, but just as they were thinking of returning to their tents and sleeping bags, the bear came back.

Eventually, it left again, leaving behind a disheveled campsite and five concerned campers.

One of the scared youngsters voiced what they were all thinking. "Let's hit the trail and head back to the lodge!"

"We'd never make it in the dark. We've only got one flash-light."

Reluctantly, they decided all they could do was go to bed and keep a roaring fire going all night, in hopes of keeping the bear at bay.

Youth is not wasted on the young, it seems, because all five campers put aside thoughts of the bear and slept. In the middle of the night, however, Denise Huckle, the other woman on the trip, thought she heard something splashing in the shallow water of the nearby lake. She tucked her dog deeper into her bag and woke the others up. They built the fire back up and set out a bag of cookies a short distance away. Jack Olsen reports, "Within a few minutes they all saw a bear walk to the edge of the camp, grab up the cookie bag in a huge paw, and disappear." By now the group was truly frightened, but all they could do was keep the fire going and wait until morning.

An hour or so later, as the fire was again burning low, the bear returned. Paul Dunn, a sixteen-year-old, heard the bear's sniffing sounds getting closer and closer and suddenly felt the bear tug on his sweatshirt. He jumped up, yelling, and sprinted to a tree, climbing high in a flash. Ron Noseck, Denise's boyfriend, knew this distraction might be their only opportunity to run to other trees, but he had to pull Denise and her dog out of her sleeping bag to get her moving. Fear has a way of making people move either very quickly or very slowly, and Denise's legs were turning to jelly. Ron shoved her up a tree, tossed the dog up, and found a tree of his own.

Ray Noseck, Ron's brother, was lying in his sleeping bag, awaiting a similar opportunity. It came when the bear headed to Michele's sleeping bag. Ron sprinted to a tree, shouting to Michele to get out of her bag and run. Soon four voices were echoing from the treetops for Michele to run. Michele, screaming, tried to unzip the zipper, but soon the bear was pulling her sleeping bag, with her in it, up the hillside. The last they heard of Michele was her scream.

Granite Park Chalet is located 10 miles north of Trout Lake. Several popular trails lead to the chalet, both from Going-to-the-Sun Road and Many Glacier, and the chalet was usually full all summer long. Not only was the chalet a historic and well-situated resting place, it also had the reputation as being a prime spot for watching grizzly bears. The reason? Garbage. The chalet's incinerator—the size of four or five shoe boxes, according to Olsen—was too small to handle the quantity of garbage its sixty-plus guests generated each day, and so garbage was often dumped into a gully behind the chalet. Nearly every night, two or more grizzly bears foraged for their dinner right behind the chalet. They ate everything they could, and when the managers of the chalet really wanted to provide a spectacle for their guests, they put out big gobs of bacon.

The popularity of the trails and the lure of bear-watching meant that hikers often arrived only to be told that there was no room at the inn. Eventually, an unauthorized campground developed about 500 yards below the chalet. Just because the campground was unofficial, however, did not mean it was unknown to the park authorities; in fact, the park service had brought in supplies for the "unofficial" campground. And it just so happened that the trail that the bears walked nightly to feed on table scraps at the chalet passed right by the campground.

On the night of August 12, 1967, the campground below Granite Park Chalet was nearly full. Some people had spread out across the vicinity so that the actual camping area was somewhat larger than usual. At approximately 1:00 A.M., a woman in the chalet heard screams and finally managed to convince her husband, a doctor, that someone in the campground was in trouble. After rousing others in the chalet, a group nervously set out to investigate the noises. What they discovered would change them and Glacier Park forever.

Roy Ducat and Julie Helgeson were employees at East Glacier Lodge. Roy was eighteen and a sophomore at Bowling Green State University, and nineteen-year-old Julie was a sophomore at the University of Minnesota. They were sweet and popular and having a great summer. They had hiked from Logan Pass and made their camp at the campground about 500 yards from the table scraps that were destined to become the bears' midnight snack. Not long after they turned in for the night, Roy was suddenly awakened by Julie whispering to him to play dead. Before he knew what was going on, he was flying through the air. He landed on his stomach, and almost immediately he felt the searing heat of something biting into his right shoulder. He knew, of course, that it had to be a bear, and before he had his wits about him he realized that the bear had left him to go to Julie. It quickly returned to Roy, again biting him on the shoulder and then beginning to attack his legs, but then the bear left again. Roy heard bones crunching and Julie screaming. With horror he realized that Julie's screams were getting fainter: She was being dragged down the hill.

Roy managed to alert some nearby campers, and soon he was receiving the medical attention he desperately needed. It took some time for his exhortations to save Julie to motivate the crew who had assembled in the middle of the night, many of whom had been awakened by the shrieking they heard from the campground. No one was keen to head off in the pitch blackness, but neither could they stomach the idea of leaving Julie alone out there, possibly alive. Finally a search party was organized and terrified, they worked their way, flaming torches in hand, through the trees surrounding the area. Nearly two hours had passed since the attack. Finally, Julie was found. She was alive, but just barely, in a condition nearly beyond description. Improbably, there were three doctors staying at the chalet, but despite their best efforts, they could not stop air from leaking through the massive puncture wounds in her chest. Julie Helgeson died at 4:12 A.M.

Park officials were hard-pressed to explain the events of the horrible night to the public. Theories came gushing from park headquarters, including one that posited that the bears had somehow gone crazy from the hundred-odd lightning strikes in the park two days before. In reality the confounding coincidence that during a four-hour period two nineteen-year-old women were killed by bears, the first two fatal maulings in the park's history, is much more complicated.

Certain conservationists and citizens were quick to point out that the park service had made mistakes over the years that had directly resulted in the tragedies. The park service had known about the bear feedings at Granite Park and made no serious effort to end them. Furthermore, they had tacitly approved the establishment of a campground in an area that had been frequented by grizzlies for decades and was bordered by a trail used nightly by bears who were going to the chalet to feed. And regarding the Trout Lake killing, a marauding bear had been allowed to terrorize campers for three months.

They also pointed to a bigger picture. Bears had been losing their habitat to humans for more than a hundred years. Grizzlies, who had once roamed the plains, had retreated to the highest and most formidable mountains in the region in an attempt to get away from humans, but now people were even coming there. It is against the nature of the grizzly to want to be near humans, but when enough come close, and almost all of them with food, their normal state of aversion naturally becomes unbalanced.

Beyond the business of pointing fingers, many people, but not all, agreed that the bears had to be killed. In the days following the deaths of Michele and Julie, three bears were killed at Granite Park Chalet, and one was killed at Trout Lake.

Bear encounters continue at Glacier. The chance to see a bear is one of the reasons people come to the park, and actually catching a glimpse of one can be the defining moment of a summer's visit. It is an honor to share the mountains with these awesome animals; however, their space continues to shrink as more and more hikers penetrate the backcountry of Glacier. Even as bears have to do more to avoid contact with hikers, the park service has done more to enforce the rules that protect both humans and bears. For instance, trails may be closed when bears are spotted. Likewise, campgrounds are closed when grizzlies are known to be staying in the area. And perhaps most important, there is a strict "pack in, pack out" policy regarding all food and trash.

Tragedy on Mount Cleveland
· 1969 ·

Only those young men who dare to challenge shall
ever really accomplish.

—George Ostrom, quoted in
The White Death by McKay Jenkins

In the final days of December in 1969, five boys challenged
Mount Cleveland (10,449 feet), Glacier's highest peak. The fact
that their effort ended in wholesale tragedy should not be the
definitive assessment of their endeavor. History would be re-
miss not to highlight their daring, courage, and accomplish-
ments, as well as the bravery of the teams that risked their lives
in the subsequent search and recovery efforts.

Ray Martin and Clare Pogreba, both twenty-two-year-old
Montana Tech students from Butte who had begun their
school's climbing club, were the oldest climbers in the group.
The other members of the expedition included Montana State
University students Jerry Kanzler, eighteen, from Columbia
Falls; Mark Levitan from Helena, also eighteen; and James Anderson, twenty, from Bigfork. Young though they may have
been, none was inexperienced. All were fully aware of the dangers inherent in their undertaking.

Jerry Kanzler was particularly familiar with climbs in the park. Ever since he and his older brother, Jim, were young boys, they had gone on countless hiking and climbing expeditions with their father, Hal. A vigorous, tough old Marine, Hal's infectious appreciation for the outdoors was passed on to his young sons. Because of Hal's inspiration and their own blossoming skills, the two young Kanzler boys became known by the 1960s as a pair of the state's best young climbers.

Many family photographs document the Kanzler trips, taken on windswept ridges, sharp peaks, and along countless mountainside trails, testifying to the scope of the Kanzler boys' experience. In several photos Mount Cleveland looms in the background, foreshadowing Jerry's ultimate fate.

At fourteen Jerry took a trip to Washington and Oregon. Within a single week he climbed Mount Hood, Mount Adams, and Mount St. Helens, easily the highest mountains in the region. At seventeen, when most boys do well to navigate a car through a parking lot, Jerry scaled the Grand Teton's north ridge and called it "easy." Jerry was no amateur.

The second member of the expedition was Ray Martin. Tall and skinny, Ray towered over his climbing companions. While in his late teens, Ray spent summers in Alaska working as a firefighter. By 1969 he was back in the Great North, tackling a job that would give most people heart attacks but one that Ray found thrilling: climbing giant radio towers to inspect and install communications equipment for the Federal Electric Corporation.

McKay Jenkins, in his book *The White Death,* which documents this attempt to scale Mount Cleveland, reported Ray's answer to his mother's concerns regarding his risky employment, "Mom, if you had your way I would never get off the couch. I would just sit at home and never get outside. When my time comes to go, it could be walking across the street or whatever, so don't worry all the time. You can't control destiny, 'cause I'm going to live my life to the fullest."

Ray Martin met Clare Pogreba in junior high, and the two became fast friends, especially since Clare had a similar obsession with climbing. At Montana Tech Clare became known for practicing ice climbing by flooding ramps at the football stadium during cold weather. Clare had hoped to join the U.S. Army, but foot problems kept him out of the military. These troubles in no way kept him off mountains, however. Not only did Clare spend plenty of time hiking and climbing the mountains of Montana, he planned to join the Peace Corps after he graduated from college in 1970 and go to Nepal. The idea of being next door to the Himalayas was too much to resist. But before leaving the country, Clare wanted to climb Mount Cleveland.

The fourth member of the team was Mark Levitan. Eager and intelligent, Mark approached mountain climbing as a thrilling lesson in problem solving. The mechanical challenges of technical climbing were hands-on equations crying out for a solution. On one of their trips, Mark and his father had successfully scaled Wyoming's Grand Teton with the National Outdoor Leadership School. Mark was a natural, and while at the school, he became friends with another climber named James Anderson.

A natural athlete who had excelled at high school football and track, James tried his hand at climbing and found a new love. Described as scholarly "beyond the run of young men of his age," James took a philosophical approach to climbing. James's old scoutmaster said, "The only reprimand I ever gave the boy in five years of scouting was for being too brave. What a wonderful flaw!"

During the summer of 1969, the five young men made plans for something that had yet to be accomplished: a winter ascent of Mount Cleveland's north face. This effort was dangerous for multiple reasons. First was the obvious hazard of inclement weather. When mountain climbing in winter, a sudden storm at a high altitude may be enough to bring an expedition to a tragic end. Furthermore, Glacier's sedimentary rock is excessively fractured and brittle. Robert Madsen, an experienced climber with climbs throughout all of North America, states in *The White Death* that he has been "more frightened climbing that crap in Glacier than 3,200 feet of granite in Yosemite." Additionally, Mount Cleveland's remote location meant it was accessible only through a difficult hike after crossing the lake by boat. But the single largest factor contributing to the extreme risk of this venture was the boys' decision to tackle Mount Cleveland's north face, a dizzying vertical pitch of nearly 4,000 feet.

The north-face pitch had never been climbed in winter. Two experienced climbers, Tom Nichols and Marshall Gingery, had tried it in September 1956, but the two made it only to one of the higher ridges. J. Gordon Edwards, the author of Glacier's definitive climbing guide, traveled to the base in the summer before the boys' expedition to judge conditions for a winter climb and flatly decided it was impossible. It was this "impossible route" that the boys had decided they must take—what challenge could the alternate, western ridge route serve if they were following in the footprints of others? After all, James Anderson and his brother Bud had already accomplished that route twice before—where was the stunning triumph in merely repeating an "easy climb" in winter?

The boys sought the counsel of ranger Bob Frauson, an experienced climber in his own right and also a past member of the Tenth Mountain Division, the famed division of mountain soldiers who fought in World War II and smashed the German army lines by taking Mount Belvedere and Riva Ridge. In a *Great Falls Tribune* article of January 23, 2000, marking the tenth anniversary of the tragedy, Ranger Frauson recalled his warnings: "They wanted to do the north face and I told them that was bad. I didn't want to tell them what to do—that makes people want to go somewhere all that much more—so I tried to explain the conditions and terrain." The huge, bare parabola of the north face, he cautioned, "is like an escalator with avalanches coming down." The boys considered his advice but decided to rely on their skill and bravado. The day after Christmas in 1969, they told Frauson not to worry unless they didn't return by noon on January 2.

On New Year's Eve, veteran pilot Bud Anderson (the older brother of James) took a flight over the area to check on the young men's progress and caught sight of footprints leading across the lower reaches of the western face. He was concerned to see that the tracks ended at the clear edge of a fresh avalanche about halfway up. He also thought he spied other tracks leading away from the debris on the other side and optimistically concluded that the slide had happened after the danger area had been passed.

All those with knowledge of the boys' mission were faced with justifiable worry as the weather deteriorated after their departure. When January 2 arrived and the boys had not yet returned, searchers set out. The rescue party consisted of a few family friends and rangers from both Glacier and Waterton National Parks, including Bob Frauson. After tromping through new-fallen snow and declining temperatures, they came upon the boys' camp at the base of the mountain. Oddly, the searchers found a still-smoldering fire at the camp and quite a bit of equipment scattered about. Two sets of tracks led away: One set toward the easier west slope and another set heading straight up toward the north face. Speculation was widespread: The abandoned gear may just have been extra weight they wanted to avoid on the actual climb, but why had they split up? Did some balk at the north face and decide on the west instead? Were they planning to regroup farther up? Unfortunately, scores of overlapping mountain goat tracks obliterated both sets of tracks at the mountain's base.

The park service had major concerns with allowing Jerry's brother Jim and family friends Pat Callis and Peter Lev—all with impressive experience as technical climbers—to join in the search and possibly get into trouble of their own. Furthermore, the National Weather Service was warning that a major storm front was expected to enter the area within twelve hours. Nevertheless, the Callis-Lev-Kanzler team prevailed and was allowed to follow the west-face tracks while others followed the north.

As the weather deteriorated and night fell, the west-face team was radioed to return, but they somehow didn't receive the orders (or perhaps it is safe to assume they ignored them) until it was too late to turn back, and they were forced to spend a frigid, windswept night at about 7,000 feet. Conversation that night circled around what they had noticed that day: The mild winter up to that point had left deceptively little snow at the base and on the mountain; the sheer cliffs looked dry; and the dangerous snow loads on the successive shelves were impossible to see until it was too late. The next day, as they began to traverse the west bowl, they spotted what they thought could have claimed the young men: a massive snow-fracture line, indicating an avalanche, some 3 feet deep and stretching nearly half a mile across the bowl. With sinking hearts they realized that a giant slab avalanche had broken off sometime in the days past and had crashed down the mountain.

On January 5 they found a small backpack and a camera. When the film was developed, it provided eerie shots—photos of the boys on their trip in and at the base camp—but no solid clues. By January 9, despite a huge search effort including military helicopters, no other clues had been found. Then a major storm hit, making further search impossible until spring.

The terrible mystery continued through the interminable winter months. By May family friends and rangers were back on-site, braving frequent rockfalls and late-season avalanches. More gear began to surface, spread out over a mile-and-a-half area.

The staff of the National Park Service did their best to keep unofficial searchers out of the area. They were particularly nervous about George Ostrom, local broadcaster for KOFI radio, famed columnist and newspaperman, wildlife photographer, and a shoot-from-the-hip Glacier Park patriarch who pulled no punches when criticizing the park service when he felt criticism was deserved. Just two years before, he had (many believe justifiably) blasted the park service for the foolish policies and lack of common sense that triggered the now-infamous "Night of the Grizzlies" in which two people lost their lives in separate bear attacks in the park. Ostrom's efforts showed it was human stupidity at fault for the tragic debacle, not ferocious man-eating monster bears. The park service had enough on its hands without risking any criticism of the recovery effort.

George Ostrom happened to be a close friend of the Kanzlers, having accompanied Hal and his boys on many past hikes, and he made a solemn promise to Jerry's grieving mother that he would bring Jerry home before the grizzlies came out.

"When the park service heard I was heading for Goat Haunt, the director called and tried to tell me to stay away," Ostrom recalls. "I told them I made a promise to Jerry's mother and I'd like to see him stop me." When Ostrom stepped off the boat from Waterton, there was a ranger waiting for him. He didn't try to stop Ostrom but served as an official escort to watch over things.

Together, they searched the lower slopes of the western bowl. By this time the huge snowfield at the bottom was slowly melting. A small waterfall cascaded over the successive ledges, and Ostrom climbed up over the shelves while the scowling ranger watched from below, unwilling to risk the persistent rockfalls that eventually turned them back. Although he didn't know it, Ostrom had been within yards of the hidden boys.

Two days later, a group of rangers decided to try another inspection of the upper-bowl shelves. They climbed up to 6,800 feet to a large, flat area along the same waterfall that Ostrom had traveled. Above this, the stream gushed from beneath a hollow in the melting snowpack. Jack Christiansen, thirsty from the vigorous climb, knelt down at the mouth of the tunnel for a drink from the cold creek and caught an unmistakable odor. The searchers shined a flashlight into the wet tunnel. To their horror they saw a pair of arms and a head dangling down from the roof into the meltwater. Ray Martin had been found.

Within three difficult days the bodies of the rest of the boys had been exhumed from the snowpack. Ray had been roped to Jerry Kanzler, found 70 feet upslope. Thirty feet farther on, Jim Anderson was found, similarly roped to Mark Levitan and Clare Pogreba, themselves lying buried just a few feet above Jerry.

The rescue effort was hard enough emotionally, but the site conditions were worse. The recovery team was forced to resort to hand digging a 58-foot-long, sometimes 25-foot-deep trench to recover the bodies. Rockfalls posed ever-present danger. Scavenging bears lurked, hungry from hibernation. Once, while using a rescue toboggan to slide snow out from the trench, the toboggan got away from the team and zoomed straight for superintendent William Briggles, standing near the edge of the ledges. Had he not jumped aside at the last second, Briggles would have been knocked over the cliff.

Friends and family finally got confirmation of what they had suspected: A sudden, massive slab avalanche had overtaken the group. With a leaden heart George Ostrom arrived at the site and fulfilled his promise by bringing Jerry home and sealing the coffin, thus sparing Jerry's mother a task best left to others.

The Mount Cleveland expedition resulted in the largest single loss of life in Glacier National Park. To some people it is also the single largest act of courage and daring. Perhaps the spirit of the effort was best captured at James Anderson's memorial by the officiant, who fittingly called to mind the American Indian spiritual link to the grand mountains: "Here the Great Spirit dwells and inspires me to do great things."

Hollywood Invades Glacier

·1979·

Heaven's Gate is probably the most notorious
movie flop of all time.

> —James Kendrick, film reviewer

To Hell with Heaven's Gate.

> —Bumper sticker in the
> Flathead Valley of Montana, 1979

Writer/director Michael Cimino's movie *The Deer Hunter*
swept the 1978 Oscars. With such accolades bolstering his confidence, Cimino planned to make an epic-sweeping western, hoping it would win similar commendation. *Heaven's Gate,* despite its Wyoming setting, would use the grand scenic backdrops of Glacier National Park for many key scenes, guaranteeing that the movie would blow away audiences with magnificent landscapes alone. Big plans, big effects, big cast—big disaster.

When production began in 1979, careful arrangements were made between Cimino's production organization and the National Park Service. Filming locations included the Burlington Northern railroad tracks on the south side of the park, a shack at the head of Appekunny Creek, the North Fork Flathead River, Many Glacier, and the Two Medicine area, which would be turned into the fictional town of Sweetwater, Wyoming.

Unfortunately, from the National Park Service's perspective, things went wrong almost from the start, especially at the Two Medicine area. To create the movie town of Sweetwater, crews had to construct several period buildings, cover parking lots with dirt, screen out established structures, and make thousands of other small modifications to the area so that it would look "authentically" western. Two Medicine witnessed the highest incidence of bustling humanity in its history.

Movie crews started drilling holes in the parking lot to set up equipment and scene supports on May 1. By the time filming began on May 24, the Two Medicine area was unrecognizable. Local residents and park patrons were not happy.

"I was absolutely appalled at the thousands of tons of material and equipment they had brought in there," wrote Wilbur P. Werner of Cut Bank to the *Hungry Horse News* on June 14. "I do not feel that the area can ever be restored to its original condition. The physical effects of crowds of people, equipment, heavy machinery, buildings, props, some eighty-five horses and concentrated numbers of interested onlookers will have a devastating effect for years to come. . . . They have created a movie-maker's idea of a Wyoming town, not related to Montana, to be created in Glacier National Park. To use our park like this to me is almost sacrilegious."

Was granting permission to film in a sensitive ecosystem inside a national park a mistake? Originally, park officials didn't think so. In a July 14, 1979, interview in the *Hungry Horse News,* Philip Iversen, the park's superintendent, indicated that "the original motivation for letting Cimino film in Glacier was based on giving people all over the world an opportunity to see the park. There were no other benefits, financial or otherwise. We weren't looking for any."

Nonetheless, having many hundreds of cast and crew members, along with props and technical equipment, in such a limited, delicate area like Two Medicine may have precluded ever having a happy ending. As Iversen reported, "By nature, I'm an optimist. I didn't foresee any difficulty in managing them. The problem was not the people but the basic group structure. There was difficulty in trying to manage the organization because there were so many bosses and no central coordination. We would tell one person not to do one thing and we'd come back and find someone else had done the opposite."

Jim Burnett, resource management ranger, identified several specific problems the park service had with the way filming was conducted. He noted that crew members had driven and parked on highly sensitive areas, had thrown food and garbage on the ground, had used the surrounding woods for toilet purposes, and had driven wagons into an "off-limits area" for one particular scene. Simply restoring the vegetation would be a very expensive and time-consuming project for the park.

Iversen sent Cimino a letter ordering him to cancel all future filming at Two Medicine and the North Fork in order to protect the delicate areas and prevent any further destruction. Needless to say, Cimino was not happy. One of the forbidden locations was slated for a meadow baseball scene as well as large sequences involving fifty mercenaries and horses. Now he would have to find alternate locations. Cimino called a press conference at Kalispell's Outlaw Inn to blast Iversen publicly, accusing him of developing "the same isolation President Nixon exhibited in his Oval office."

Cimino continued, "We have kept our written agreement with Glacier National Park . . . . We have cleared the park as of June 10 according to that contract. We have removed all sets, done the rehabilitation work, lived up to every point in our written agreement. . . . I don't know what else we could have done. I simply cannot understand the degree of isolation with which Iversen has surrounded himself. . . . All of the areas in which we worked were already termed distress areas by park personnel. What did we really disturb? How could we, a company of 300 or so, in the park in a period of a few weeks do as much damage as they said we did compared to the damage of millions of visitors' feet tramping the park each year?"

One can only imagine Superintendent Iversen's thoughts as he sat down to read the morning paper and found Cimino's accusations. The same day the article appeared, park ranger Jim Burnett followed up on his earlier findings regarding the damage caused by the crew and put together a memorandum to the chief ranger on the subject of the *Heaven's Gate* movie activities:

> In view of the recent statements by Mr. Cimino concerning the park's position, it may be appropriate to clarify several items. While we obviously do not want to get into a "shouting match" in the press with the film industry, I do think we owe it to the public to comment on several untruths in the June 11, 1979 article in the *Daily Interlake*. . . . Mr. Cimino is quoted as saying, "We have kept our written agreement with Glacier National Park" [but] the foregoing statements are untrue. Considerable work remains on removal of construction materials and no rehabilitation work has begun at Two Medicine. As of 24 hours after the expiration of the permit deadline, it is still not possible to launch a boat at the Two Medicine boat ramp, driving onto the parking lot is hazardous due to piles of logs and dirt and a number of nails left over from the set construction, and unfilled holes in the lot are a hazard to vehicles and pedestrians. . . .
>
> Visitation to the site of the movie set runs in the tens of thousands, not millions annually. More important, these visitors do not use front end loaders and heavy tractor trailers on areas off of roadways;

they do not stand or move around in groups of "300 or so," along with dozens of horses and wagons, for periods of up to 12 hours a day during a two week period. Most important, the majority of visitor foot traffic is confined to the paved walks and drives in the area under discussion. . . .

One of the basic stipulations of the company's permit was that movie activities would not impair visitor use of the area. However, there were continuous conflicts between the visitors' legitimate desire to see "what was going on" in the park and film company's desire for absolute privacy. Most problems were resolved by tactful handling of complaints by park staff . . . the company's requirements for secrecy during daylight hours when filming was not underway was certainly excessive, and do not seem to comply with the provisions of the permit.

The film crew continued the cleanup at the Two Medicine site, supervised by park service members throughout the summer of 1979. On July 12 Iversen wrote Production Manager Charlie Okun that he was pleased with the results in restoring the area. After final parking lot repairs were finished in October, the cleanup was deemed complete, and the park returned the movie company's $50,000 bond.

So after all the controversy, hoopla, and restorative efforts, what was the end result? Before the movie was shown to the public, the only fact that was well known about it was its price tag: Though production costs were originally planned to be around $7 million, the final cost was a reported $43 million. Steven Bach wrote in *Final Cut: Art, Money, and Ego in the Making of Heaven's Gate, the Film that Sank United Artists* that after enduring "Cimino's egomaniacal delays, refusals to work within budgetary constraints (he never even signed-off on the actual budget agreement) and refusal to let his bosses even see a single snippet of film, United Artists was left with an original 'final cut' of *Heaven's Gate.* The flick came in at five-and-a-half hours, was deemed unwatchable by even the most optimistic viewers and finally ruined the studio that had been cofounded by Charlie Chaplin. Now that's a disaster film."

In 1997 film reviewer James Kendrick called it "probably the most notorious movie flop of all time. . . . The nearly four-hour epic western was so savaged by critics at its New York premiere, that the producers pulled it and cut out a third of the film before issuing it into wide release. With nearly an hour missing, the already confusing story was made literally incomprehensible, and the rest is history. . . . Even though *Heaven's Gate* is an often visually arresting movie filmed on beautiful locations in England and Wyoming [Kendrick didn't know that the Wyoming stuff had actually been filmed in Montana] . . . the movie flounders and eventually collapses under its own weight."

The film was not without its fans, although in limited numbers. Linda Heard, a reviewer for the *Detroit Free Press,* wrote in 1999: "The film knocked me out. I thought the acting outstanding, the story fascinating and the cinematography stunning. Despite critics' pans, *Heaven's Gate* became my favorite film."

Heaven's Gate was officially released in 1980 and starred Kris Kristofferson, Christopher Walken, Isabelle Huppert, John Hurt, Sam Waterston, Brad Dourif, Joseph Cotten, and Jeff Bridges. The movie is available today on VHS and DVD. Fortunately, Glacier Park survived this encounter with Hollywood and is also still available, in full and living color.

The Spirits Listen
· 1991 ·

The Spiritual Powers that attracted the People of
the Past are as strong today as they were then.

—Adolf Hungry Wolf,
Good Medicine in Glacier National Park

Some people say it was God's will; others say it was clear
evidence of the spirits that still reside within Glacier's borders.
Perhaps it was nothing more complicated than human courage
in the leering face of death. Whatever force is credited, there
is no denying that what two Michigan tourists experienced on
the cool afternoon of August 30, 1991, was nothing short of
miraculous.

Deane and Lorraine Lengkeek, residents of Holland,
Michigan, were enthralled as they enjoyed the incredible vistas
of Glacier National Park on their self-described "dream vacation." This was their time to enjoy themselves after successfully
raising five children and assisting in raising fifteen grandkids.
"This was the adventure of a lifetime," Lorraine later wrote in
Guideposts magazine, "to be out on our own in nature with no
one around for miles and all the time in the world." And so
they found themselves in Glacier backcountry, hiking back
from Iceberg Lake in the Many Glacier Valley.

They were aware of the backcountry dangers, particularly
the potential for an encounter with a grizzly. Having rejected

bear bells, Lorraine loudly sang out "How Great Thou Art," her favorite hymn, to proclaim their presence and faith. As they advanced down the trail, their mood was light and carefree. Lorraine had only one slight anxiety: that her husband, a diabetic, would get a hearty supper after their earlier light lunch. Around the next curve, however, they faced the possibility of being the main course.

They had no warning—the huge bear (whether it was a grizzly or black bear is still a matter of debate) was simply there, "teeth bared, clawing at the sky." Worse yet, a pair of young cubs scampered at the bear's feet, instantly identifying the bear as a protective mother. There was no time to perform the tuck-and-drop the park rangers had suggested. The bruin immediately charged. The roaring mother bear quickly seized Deane and tossed him into the air. Then the bear grabbed his arm and threw him again. When Deane smashed into the ground a second time, the bear chomped into one of his legs.

Nearly overwhelmed by the sight, Lorraine nevertheless remembered the rangers' advice: Drop; cover your neck with interlaced hands; keep down; stay still. She knew those techniques were her best strategy to survive. But the rangers had said nothing about what to do while your husband was being mauled. Lorraine responded with gut instinct. The 130-pound grandmother rushed in like a tag-team wrestler.

"Let go of my husband!" Lorraine rushed at the bear and began to pound her binoculars into its enormous snout. She reported that "her powerful jaws opened and closed. I felt her breath hot and moist on my face." Still she whacked the bear, her arm aching with the effort. "Then, as I prepared for one final blow, the bear abruptly released Deane, dropped to all fours and retreated, snarling and panting." The bruin and her cubs were gone.

Lorraine huffed in exhaustion and relief—until she looked at her husband. Deane lay still, conscious but brutally injured by both tooth and claw. "His face was ashen, his arm mangled, his body smeared with blood." The physical trauma was bad enough, but with his diabetic condition, Deane was in a precarious situation. He was unable to speak when he tried.

"Help! Somebody help us!" Lorraine started screaming. There was no response, just the beautiful and uncaring silence of the upper Many Glacier Valley. They were an impossible 4 miles from camp. There was no way Lorraine could get Deane down the trail and to medical care. Lorraine's dream vacation had now turned into a life-or-death nightmare. "I glanced at my watch. I had once heard that the sixty minutes after an accident are the most crucial—the Golden Hour, emergency room doctors call it. With proper help people can survive even the gravest injuries." But Deane was far, far away from the nearest emergency room, and his lifeblood was seeping out of him.

Lorraine knew she had to try to stop the bleeding. With great ingenuity she used her elastic bra to fashion a tourniquet for Deane's arm and used cloth scraps and tissues to pack the largest wounds on his chest. "I noticed Deane's hand was swelling due to the tourniquet. I slipped off his wedding band, then released some pressure on his arm. It was the first time in our forty-three-year marriage the ring had left his finger. I scrounged around the pack for our water bottle. I lifted Deane's head and gave him the last drink."

Lorraine felt Deane start to shiver in her arms. "God," she implored, "we are all alone. Without you, my husband will die." The spirits listened.

Just as Lorraine screamed for help again, she heard a voice calling back. Two young men hurried up the trail. They quickly assessed the situation and promptly covered Deane with a sweatshirt and propped up his feet with a backpack. Lorraine was searching her mind for next steps when one of the young men declared in a German accent, "I am a distance runner. I'll go for help." With that startling declaration he dashed off down the trail.

It seemed God or the Glacier spirits had delivered a small miracle, but Lorraine knew that Deane needed more care than she and this other park visitor could provide.

Seconds later, a young couple came down the trail. To Lorraine's astonishment the woman announced she was a nurse. She went to work on Deane, monitoring his vital signs, giving him more water, and even administering a painkiller.

Soon another hiker came along. His contributions were a crucial foil survival blanket to keep Deane warm and sterile bandages for the wounds. Deane was clearly receiving better care than he had been just moments before, but his face was getting paler, and diabetes-exacerbated shock was obviously setting in. He could barely murmur his request for something to eat as his blood sugar plummeted.

"Can we help?" Another couple had arrived on the scene. Before Lorraine could finish explaining that her husband was a diabetic, the woman—unbelievably, another nurse—had instantly retrieved an orange from her friend's pack. Short of a shot of real insulin, it was exactly what was needed to boost Deane's glucose levels.

Other people began to arrive, trickling in until there was quite a crowd, including one vacationing Israeli Army commando. He quickly assessed the situation, considered the next steps that would need to be taken, and mapped out a plan of action. Dispatching one of the couples down the trail to make sure the distance runner hadn't been waylaid, he then organized the remaining hikers and instructed them to begin clearing brush and young pines to create a landing spot for a rescue helicopter. This was difficult work as the only tools the group had consisted of six pocketknives, but the commando knew that all the previous efforts to save Deane would be for naught if a helicopter couldn't land to retrieve him.

As the group hacked away at the trees and underbrush, the couple who had gone to check on the German runner returned with a ranger, who had started up the trail after the runner had found him. The ranger was impressed by the forward-thinking group and their efforts to clear an area for a helicopter. Lorraine's relief was evident as the ranger reported that a rescue helicopter was indeed on its way, and he quickly radioed the group's position to the pilot, who was waiting for the call. The group marked the spot with a sheet of shiny, reflective survival wrap to signal the pilot, and just a few minutes later, the helicopter arrived.

Deane Lengkeek reached Kalispell Regional Hospital in critical condition. After seven hours of surgery, the doctors announced that he would make a full recovery. The next ten days of Deane's "vacation" were spent in a hospital room. "God gave us exactly what we needed when we needed it," Lorraine reported afterward. Among those who had come upon the Lengkeeks, in addition to the distance runner, nurses, and army commando, were a third-year medical student, an emergency medical technician with mountain-rescue experience, and a physician.

Coincidences? Any visitor who is open to the magic of Glacier knows better. In the solitude and stillness of the Glacier backcountry, you may find that spirits are watching over you as well.

Glacier Ghosts and Haunted Hotels
• 1999 •

In the early days at Glacier National Park, most visitors arrived by rail at the town of Belton (now West Glacier). The Belton Chalet, completed in 1910, became the home away from home for most of these early tourists. By the mid-1990s, however, the chalet had been closed for half a century. There had been brief periods during which it had been transformed into a quiet pizza parlor, a bakery, and a cafe, but most of the hotel complex had stood silent—proud but cold, dark, and shuttered—since the days when the Second World War had virtually eliminated Glacier Park tourism. The construction of the Going-to-the-Sun Road also dealt a blow to business at the chalet, since it allowed visitors to drive to and through the park rather than relying on the railway. Nonetheless, after fifty years of benign neglect, the hotel was brought back to life by Andy Baxter and Cas Still, a husband and wife team from Yellow Bay, Montana, who still saw promise in the dilapidated Swiss-style hotel. In 1996 they purchased the buildings and did what they do best: restore old homes and buildings. By 1999 a grand, gorgeous, newly renovated Belton Chalet and Railroad Hotel was set to open, ready to welcome guests as it once had greeted travelers on Louis Hill's Great Northern trains.

Cindy Moore, the hotel's manager for new rooms, was helping out in that effort. It was a bright spring day outside, but winter's stale chill lingered throughout the huge timber building as she worked alone. "I was setting up the front desk. I kept hearing doors slam." She was certain these weren't the sounds of car doors or banging, windblown shutters. "It was very obvious . . . boom! It was down this hall." The hall in question was on the second floor, a lovely passage with high ceilings, gracefully suspended light globes, and plenty of wood accenting modern, comfortable accommodations, maintaining their original 1910 style.

Moore went to investigate. Halfway down the hall, she suddenly felt as though she had crossed an invisible line and walked into an "ice-cold" chill. It was as if she had walked through a doorway into a cold room, but she was still standing in the charming hotel corridor. Not sure how to explain the sudden change in temperature but very sure she didn't want to be up there alone, she returned to her work at the front desk and tried to ignore the feeling in the pit of her stomach. The phantom, however, wasn't content to leave her in peace and be ignored. The sound of banging doors did not diminish. "I was freaked at that point, so I didn't go back [up there]. I finished up my work and got out. But I knew there was something there at the end of the hall."

On a later day Moore was again tending the front desk when she became aware that behind and above her right shoulder, something began to move on the staircase. "Suddenly, the light fixture above the staircase began to swing back and forth." There was no wind and no drafts to explain the pendulum movement of the light fixture. No freights rumbled by on the train tracks outside. No heavy highway traffic or wayward earthquake—just one wildly swinging light fixture and a very spooky feeling for Cindy.

Is the Belton Chalet and Railroad Hotel haunted? To Cindy Moore the answer is clear. Furthermore, many past guests and most employees have their own stories to lend credence to hers. Even Cas Still and Andy Baxter had reason to wonder.

They eventually consulted with Curly Bear Wagner, a Blackfeet cultural interpreter, who performed a cleansing ceremony, which is reported to have brought a calm over the building by honoring its spirits.

But to other people, such as historian Bob Jacobs, the creepy happenings and ghostly sightings reported at Belton are nothing but a bunch of foolishness. After all, despite diligent research, Jacobs can't identify a single tragic event associated with the hotel, chalets, past owners, or staff. "That's why it can't be haunted," according to Jacobs. "No murders, suicides, or other dramatic event to give reason for any hauntings in the first place." Of course, there is one dreadful tale of a poor young newlywed who arrived unexpectedly on an early train only to find her roguish groom shacked up at the hotel with his illicit mistress. Racked with grief, the spurned bride responded by throwing herself to her death off the top of a nearby cliff (the huge, 85-or-so-foot-high rock outcropping referred to as "the Reef," located above the present-day west parking lot).

According to Bob Jacobs that's still not a good enough story to presume a haunting, especially since he claims he made up the shafted bride story himself. "I'm embarrassed that it was taken so seriously," Jacobs says, admitting that his tale gained instant acceptance within a matter of days and even appeared as accepted legend within a local Flathead Valley newspaper. "It either goes to show the power of rumor or my credibility as a historian."

The Belton Hotel is not the only one in Glacier rumored to have invisible guests. At the Prince of Wales Hotel in Waterton, on the Canadian side of the International Peace Park, a parallel story is told of the ghostly apparition of Sarah, a summer employee who reportedly fell from a window and now haunts the halls of the grand hotel. Sarah is said to roam the corridors, frightening staff and guests alike with her moans and wails. A different version of the story identifies Sarah not as a summer employee but as a new bride, who similarly discovered her groom with a mistress. According to this version she jumped out of the highest window on the hotel's lakeside face.

Leon Stiffarm, director of human resources at Glacier Park, Inc., noted in a February 28, 2002, interview in Kalispell's *Daily InterLake* newspaper that ghosts are said to inhabit Glacier Park Lodge in East Glacier, as well as Many Glacier Hotel. Activity is supposed to peak during times of low visitation, such as the beginning and end of tourist seasons. "Some of our housekeepers don't like to be in the rooms alone. There's a lot of real damp, cold feelings in some of the rooms at Glacier Park Lodge. But then I always remind people that it's a hundred-year-old lodge with real bad heat."

Back at the Belton Hotel, Stiffarm's pragmatic comments don't offer much comfort to the staff. For example, consider the young man who had to work a call-in nightshift at Belton Hotel's front desk. "When I showed up early the next morning," Cindy Moore reports, "he was standing, freezing, on the front porch with keys in hand. He gave up the keys and said that was the last time he was going to work that shift." He never explained to Cindy what he had felt or witnessed; he simply refused to work the nightshift again. Soon after that, the regular night auditor quit after only a few days. Somewhere off in the darkness, he could hear footsteps or a little girl softly crying. At other times, as with virtually all the staff, he would hear his name being whispered—urgently, harshly, and softly.

The spirits don't seem to be content to stay in just one wing of the Belton Hotel. Cooks have reported hearing clanging pots and pans. Witnesses have seen lights turning on and off on their own throughout the hotel. A man's soft cries are sometimes heard in the upstairs hallways. On several occasions the sociable murmurings of a busy bar can be heard up above the Grill & Tap Room—when the restaurant is dark and closed. The hotel dog refuses to go near the taproom. Yet the spirit appears to be friendly enough. Moore says that when things get too noisy, she just tells it to keep quiet. "Then he settles down," she says casually.

Perhaps the most striking supernatural experience at the Belton happened to a female guest from Texas in 1999. She had not heard the slightest rumor of any hauntings, and spooky phantoms were the last thing on her mind. Standing in the far corner of Room 27, engrossed in a cell-phone call, she casually turned to face the door and was startled to see she was not alone. A ghostly apparition stood glowing across the room.

According to Cindy Moore, "She couldn't see the feet really, but she saw the rest of him." Moore goes on to say that the guest described the apparition as that of an older man wearing turn-of-the-twentieth-century clothes. "Long, brown suit. Thin black tie and a derby hat. Then, the thing—whatever it was—slowly turned and looked right at her. The ghost made direct eye contact with our guest." Later, the woman pointed to a picture of railroad magnates Louis and James Hill, claiming they closely resembled the spirit. As this same specter has also been seen at the restaurant and train depot, there's some thought that the ghost(s) may be that of the brothers who originally built the Belton Chalet.

It would be fitting if the Belton spirits were the Hills. Belton was undoubtedly the primary destination for park visitors arriving by railroad, especially in 1910, the year Glacier was dedicated as a national park and the Hill brothers built the hotel and chalet. Since Andy Baxter and Cas Still began their restoration, which won an award from the National Trust for Historic Preservation, the Belton Chalet and Railroad Hotel has reestablished itself as a landmark destination for Glacier visitors. The Grill Dining Room is said to feature some of the finest food in the Flathead Valley, prepared in a unique outdoor kitchen on the Belton Boiler BBQ, a huge, 8-foot-long boiler tank. Comfortable rooms and good eats—perhaps it's no wonder that guests come, including the long-term sort that don't sign the register and come out only at night.

The Reds Return
· 2002 ·

Introduced in 1936, the Glacier Reds, as the park's old-fashioned touring buses are known, are the longest running fleet of passenger vehicles in U.S. history. Many factors contributed to this, not the least of which was the unique charm of these antique touring sedans. Park scenery made them remarkable travel favorites: When climate permitted—and frequently when it did *not*—the bus drivers, known around the park as jammers, would roll back the canvas tops for an awe-inspiring, full-view convertible adventure. With stunning scenic views supplemented by colorful commentary from the drivers, a Red Bus ride became one of the definitive Glacier Park tourist experiences.

Yet despite impeccable maintenance, the buses were not immune to an inevitable deterioration. As time passed, more and more mechanical ingenuity was required just to keep them rolling. The Reds were fighting a losing battle against the ravages of time. And even when they were running perfectly, they still seemed a little rickety to those people who knew and loved them. Just ask Maxson Slater (not his real name), a jammer in the mid-1980s who had a love-hate relationship with his bus. A typical story from his years on the job provides a clue about the state the Reds were in.

"Ever seen the movie *The Gods Must Be Crazy?*"

The man asking this question was smiling as he watched Slater haul a large chunk of rock out from under Red Bus 98's driver's seat and shove the big slab behind the left front tire, as was his usual practice. Content with his improvised parking brake, Slater was now free to regard the talking passenger. "Pardon me?"

"*The Gods Must be Crazy*. Ever see it?"

"No. But I've heard about it. Low-budget comedy, right?"

"Yep." The tourist chuckled. Before turning to join the other passengers admiring Jackson Glacier, he offered one small bit of puzzling advice: "Go see it sometime."

Years later, Slater saw the movie. He didn't remember the long-ago passenger's comment until he viewed a scene in which the hapless hero—in the best tradition of Lucille Ball slapstick—also used a chunk of rock for a parking brake but with far more chaotic results.

"Don't get me wrong," Slater stresses. "If I had any feeling that my Red was dangerous, I'd have had it back to East Glacier without hesitation. I just didn't . . . *trust* . . . the parking brake that I had and merely thought a little supplemental insurance sure couldn't hurt." The Reds were safe, he declares, "just a mite ragged by that time in their careers." After all, they had been in service for more than sixty-five years.

The Reds were first introduced in 1936, soon after the opening of Going-to-the-Sun Road. Manufactured by the White Truck Company, the buses were able to fit seventeen to twenty-one passengers on their long, leather bench seats and performed an integral role in the government's program to standardize passenger transportation in the national parks. About 500 of these unique open-topped touring sedans were produced for several western parks. Similar buses wowed tourists in Yellowstone and Grand Canyon.

The other parks eventually eliminated their fleets, and the Glacier Reds became one of the many unique features found only at Glacier. A few of the buses from Yellowstone (appropriately painted a bright canary yellow) found their way into Glacier's fleet; a few others fell into private hands. At least one found its way to Hollywood and can be seen in the movie *Big*

Trouble in Little Tokyo. Popular they were; indestructible they weren't. In 1999 a panel of experts examined eight of the remaining thirty-three buses and reported that serious structural problems, including fatigued and failing engine mounts, undersized brake pads, fatigued steering components, dangerous side-mounted fuel tanks, and cracking frame rails, plagued the vehicles. Dirty emissions added to the safety issues, and Glacier Park, Inc., was forced to retire the entire fleet. The future looked dark for the Reds. Many people believed the buses had passed into oblivion.

Visitors to the park after 1999 were saddened and disappointed not to see the hallmark Reds puttering down Glacier roads. Fifteen hardtop Dodge vans were used as replacements, but as Adeline Mayfield, a tourist from San Jose, stated after getting out of one of the vans on Logan Pass, "They aren't very good for seeing." Glacier authorities wanted to bring the Reds back. But how?

They decided to enter into a unique partnership with the nonprofit National Park Foundation, which had been created by Congress in 1967 to strengthen "the enduring connection between the American people and their national parks by raising private funds, making strategic grants, creating innovative partnerships and increasing public awareness." Glacier Park, Inc., donated the entire fleet of Reds to the National Park Foundation's Proud Partners of America's National Parks program.

Ford Motor Company joined in. The whole fleet was taken to Michigan, where a team of more than 200 professionals from several companies worked to restore the Reds. Ford funded and supervised the project. Transportation Design and Manufacturing (TDM) of Livonia, Michigan, was charged with performing the actual modifications and testing the new systems with the help of Ford engineers. ASG Renaissance provided project management and engineering support. GFI Control Systems, Inc., designed a new, supplemental propane fuel system.

The Propane Education & Research Council provided essential grant money in conjunction with Ford Motor Company in the development and construction of the new official Red Bus propane-fueling infrastructure.

The monumental task required two years of superhuman effort. "Restoring the Red Buses has been a bigger challenge than any of us imagined, but it has also been a labor of love to those involved," said Ford's director of alternative fuel vehicles Bruce Gordon. "We worked diligently to maintain the historic integrity of the buses and applied Ford's and TDM's expertise in alternative fuel vehicles and safety."

Key mechanical changes included these:

- Removing the original carbureted gas engines and replacing them with new fuel-injected 5.4-liter bi-fuel engines capable of running on either gasoline or propane. (The Reds are now 93 percent cleaner!)
- Installing a new exhaust system
- Installing new modern E-450 chassis specially modified to fit the Reds' bodies
- Replacing the old brake system with production-grade 4-wheel disc ABS systems
- Replacing all the windows with safety glass and replacing all the external lights to bring them up to current federal standards
- Restoring the buses' bodies by repairing damage; repainting; adding new fiberglass or sheet-metal components as necessary; replacing door latches, seats, and running boards; and covering the floors with new aluminum sheeting
- Adding new public-address systems

The Reds returned for a grand ceremony at Glacier Park Lodge on June 8, 2002. About 200 people attended to witness speakers from all participating organizations. An additional dignitary who participated was Blackfeet spiritual leader Clyde

Heavy Runner, who performed, in full tribal regalia, a blessing of the fleet.

In typical form Glacier weather provided a late-season blizzard for the event. Four feet of the wet white stuff fell along the Rocky Mountain Range, and courtesy bus rides had to be canceled. The promised picnic was served at the lodge's restaurant.

In spite of the bad weather, every person in attendance was smiling. The sun would break through soon enough, they knew, and the Reds would be ready to run again. As president of the National Park Foundation Jim Maddy said, "There is no more representative symbol of Glacier National Park than these classic red buses. To see them once again rolling across the Continental Divide on the spectacular Going-to-the-Sun Road is a dream come true."

A Potpourri of Glacier Facts

• In 1896 the Blackfeet tribe sold Glacier National Park's land to the U.S. government for $1,500,000. Glacier National Park was officially established in 1910.

• The park covers approximately 1.4 million acres and has more than 730 miles of trails.

• Glacier has 175 named mountains. Six of these have elevations above 10,000 feet.

• Glacier has 429 documented archaeological sites; these include more than fifty vision-quest sites.

• Montana is the only state with watersheds that replenish three oceans, thanks to Triple Divide Peak in Glacier National Park. Water flowing down the western side ends up in the Columbia River and then the Pacific Ocean. Water flowing down the eastern side drains into the Missouri River through the Mississippi Basin and on to the Gulf of Mexico. The northern Hudson Bay watershed reaches the Arctic Ocean.

• Relatively few ancient Blackfeet place names were recorded for Glacier National Park's mountains, streams, and other features, but the Blackfeet called the area itself "Backbone of the World" and "Home of the Wind Maker."

• Assuming that there weren't any earlier undocumented wandering mountain men or trappers, Finian MacDonald and two French-Canadians by the names of Michel Bourdeaux and Bepteste Buche were the first white men to enter the area, though others say it was trader and trapper Hugh Monroe who, at age seventeen, was an employee of the Hudson Bay Company and later married into the Blackfeet tribe. Rising Wolf Mountain is named for Monroe, who had a reputation for being surly right after waking up.

• Frontiersman Duncan McDonald was once transporting supplies to Canada in the 1880s when he considered—and soon abandoned—a brief side trip to check for an easier, quicker pass through the mountains. Stopping along the shores of a magnificent lake, he carved his name into a large tree. McDonald's original carving is long gone, but his mark endures as the lake, valley, and nearby creek still bear his name.

• Browning, Montana—tribal capital of the Blackfeet—is located on the plains just outside East Glacier and holds the national record for a twenty-four-hour temperature drop. The temperature plummeted 100 degrees on January 23, 1916, from forty-four degrees F to fifty-six degrees below zero.

• The pictographs in the Lake McDonald Lodge hearth and flagstones, reputed to be carved by the famous artist Charlie Russell, are simply based on his designs.

• In 1954 the difficult-to-operate Granite Park Chalets were sold by the Great Northern Railroad to the National Park Service for $1.00.

• Glacier was voted the best backcountry park in America by *Backpacker* magazine in 2000.

- Approximately two million visitors cross the park borders every year.

- Glacier National Park is actually only a portion of a larger park called Waterton–Glacier International Peace Park, which came about after a joint goodwill meeting of Rotary Clubs in 1931. Legislation passed the next year in both the United States and Canada joined the formerly independent parks. Commemorative rock cairn monuments were erected on each side of the border by Rotary International members in 1947, signifying a "dedication to peace between the two countries and the world."

- Waterton Lakes became a Canadian national park in 1895, fifteen years before Glacier was designated a national park. Waterton Lakes has about 100 miles of trails within its 29,000 acres.

- Lodgepole pine, one of Glacier's predominant tree species, is often considered a fire-dependent species because their pinecones require the heat of fire to release seeds. Thick stands of lodgepole generally indicate that a major fire has burned through the area.

- At one time there were 12 feet of open space between Divide Creek and the Divide Creek bridge above it. Erosion around the bridge has caused debris to pile up, reducing the space to a mere 18 inches.

- Going-to-the-Sun Road is approximately 52 miles (83 kilometers) long. Completed in 1932, its highest point is Logan Pass, at an altitude of 6,646 feet above sea level. The road rises 3,000 feet from the valley floor to Logan Pass.

• Going-to-the-Sun Road was featured in the long opening credits of the film *The Shining*.

• The West Side Tunnel was the first of Going-to-the-Sun's tunnels to be finished. It was completed in 1928 and is 192 feet in length. The East Side Tunnel is longer, at 408 feet, and was completed five years later in 1933. East Side Tunnel workmen were only able to dig 5 feet per day.

• The workers who constructed Going-to-the-Sun Road were paid as little as $3.00 per day.

• Almost 500,000 pounds of explosives were used to blast out Going-to-the-Sun Road.

• Snow usually closes Going-to-the-Sun Road near the end of October in an average year. The earliest opening date was May 16, 1987. Some years, the road cannot be opened until the end of June.

• There are fewer than 300 miles of "serviceable roads" for Glacier's 1,500 square miles.

• The first automobile entered Glacier in 1911. It belonged to Frank Stoop, from Kalispell, and was driven by a mechanic named Frank Wahlen, who later became chief engineer for the park. They negotiated a dirt road to its end at Lake Five, near the west entrance to the park.

• In 1912 W. A. Brewster headed the first transportation company in Glacier. It was started on the east side and called the Brewster Brothers. The early concession consisted of three stagecoaches, each drawn by four horses. The lines ran from the Midvale (East Glacier) railhead and visited camps in St.

Mary, Cut Bank, Many Glacier, and Two Medicine. A trip to Many Glacier took two days and involved an overnight stay in St. Mary.

• On August 7, 1914, Louis W. Hill and his Great Northern Railroad party were in the first automobile to drive on the new Many Glacier Road. Fred A. Noble, retired general manager of Glacier Park Transportation Company, drove the car.

• The first auto fee in the park was $1.00. Levi Bird paid the first fee as he traveled into Many Glacier Valley in 1911.

• Reds, specially designed Glacier touring buses, were first introduced in 1936.

• One empty Red rolled off the road at the Jackson Glacier lookout. Trees soon stopped its plummet, and it was easily re-covered. The actual date is a matter of dispute, but jammer lore puts it in either the late 1970s or early 1980s.

• From 1999 to 2002, $6.5 million was spent to restore the fleet of red buses.

• The Reds are the oldest operating passenger fleet in the world.

• In August 1983 Vice President George H. Bush stayed in Glacier National Park for two days. He hiked to Hidden Lake and fished for several hours but returned empty-handed.

• The town of St. Mary became Supreme Court Justice Earl Warren's favorite vacation spot. He sometimes visited twice a year. He was especially fond of the trout fishing opportunities on the Blackfeet Reservation's Duck Lake.

• The highest rate of military service per capita of any ethnic group in the United States is found among American Indians. Eleven percent of the people living in Browning, Montana, on Glacier's eastern border, are U.S. military veterans.

• Trespassers on snowmobiles are a constant problem for park rangers. One park ranger, Art Sedlack, became fed up with snowmobiles and their impact on sensitive backcountry earth. Sedlack didn't waste time writing tickets: He ordered one snowmobiler off to the side and proceeded to use his service revolver to execute the offending machine. Art got fired, but many consider him a kind of cult hero.

• The small village of Apgar on the west side of the park at the foot of Lake McDonald owes its name to Maine transplant Milo B. Apgar. He arrived to homestead the area in 1892, crossing over Marias Pass in a simple two-wheeled cart.

• The Snyder Hotel preceded Lake McDonald Lodge in 1895. Its proprietor, George Snyder, punched a road through from Belton to Apgar, where tourists could board his steamboat, the *F. I. Whitney*.

• The park has thirty-seven named glaciers.

• Grinnell Glacier (also called Salamander) is one of the park's biggest glaciers. Its ice depth is estimated to be more than 500 feet in places. In 1901 it measured 525 acres; by 1950 it had melted to 314 acres. Recessions have slowed somewhat, but at present Grinnell Glacier measures fewer than 300 acres, having shrunk approximately 43 percent in the past century.

• Sperry Glacier is the park's second-largest ice mass. It covered 810 acres in 1900. Sixty years later it had shrunk to just

285 acres, losing approximately 65 percent of its mass. The glacier continues to recede.

• Although the National Park Service no longer recommends bells as a warning device, bear bells are popular with Glacier National Park hikers. These are little metal jingle bells that can be carried on packs, belts, shoes, or a walking staff with the hope that their soft chiming may give some audible forewarning to any bears in the area. Some people claim they're useless; others swear by their effectiveness. Though the jingling can certainly warn of an advancing human hiker, the unusual sound can actually attract curious yearling black bears.

• Despite popular belief many grizzlies have no trouble climbing trees.

• The first fatal grizzly attack reported in the park happened during the infamous "Night of the Grizzlies" incident in August 1967, during which two people were killed in separate locations on the same night.

• There are no poisonous snakes in Glacier National Park.

• Before World War II the most popular way to see backcountry Glacier was via horse concession. Every season, more than 1,000 horses served ten times as many visitors.

• Wolves have historically been numerous throughout Glacier and the western United States. Most were wiped out during eradication efforts in the 1920s and 30s, and no dens were found for the next fifty years. In the early 1980s, however, wolves started migrating south from British Columbia and began recolonizing in the area of the North Fork Flathead River. A wolf den was found in Glacier in 1986. Wolves have established dens within the park almost every year since then. There have been absolutely no incidents of human injury or attack by the wolves.

• More than 145,000 acres burned during the fires of 2003, according to Tony Clark, Glacier deputy information officer. This set a record for the most destructive fire in the park's history.

• If weather patterns stay the same, many scientists believe that the park's glaciers will be completely gone by 2030.

Further Reading

Alt, David D., and Donald W. Hyndman. *Roadside Geology of the Northern Rockies*. Missoula, MT: Mountain Press, 1972.

———. *Rocks, Ice and Water—The Geology of Waterton-Glacier*. Missoula, MT: Mountain Press, 1973.

Bach, Steven. *Final Cut: Art, Money, and Ego in the Making of Heaven's Gate, the Film That Sank United Artists*. New York: Newmarket Press, 1999.

Buchholtz, C.W. *Man in Glacier*. Glacier Natural History Association, 1976.

Christopherson, Edmund. *Adventure among the Glaciers*. Missoula, MT: Earthquake Press, 1966.

Farabee, Charles R. "Butch," Jr. *Death, Daring and Disaster—Search and Rescue in the National Parks*. Niwot, CO: Roberts Rinehart, 1998.

Grant, Madison. *Early History of Glacier National Park*. Washington, DC: Government Printing Office, 1919.

Houk, Rose. *Going-to-the-Sun Road: The Story of the Highway Across Glacier Park*. Aspen, CO: Woodlands Press, 1984.

Hungry Wolf, Adolf. *Good Medicine in Glacier National Park—Inspirational Photos and Stories from the Days of the Blackfoot People*. Healdsburg, CA: Naturegraph Press, 1971.

Jenkins, McKay. *The White Death—Tragedy and Heroism in an Avalanche Zone*. New York: Random House, 2000.

Kresek, Ray. *Fire Lookouts of the Northwest.* Fairfield, WA: Ye Galleon Press, 1984.

Linderman, Frank Bird. *Recollections of Charley Russell.* Norman: University of Oklahoma Press, 1963.

Moylan, Bridget. *Glacier's Grandest—A Pictorial History of the Hotels and Chalets of Glacier National Park.* Missoula, MT: Pictorial Histories, 1995.

Olsen, Jack. *Night of the Grizzlies.* Moose, WY: Homestead Press, 1969.

Rinehart, Mary Roberts. *Through Glacier Park in 1915.* Niwot, CO: Roberts Rinehart, 1983.

Russell, Charles M. *Good Medicine, Memories of the Real West.* New York: Garden City, 1929.

Taliaferro, John. *Charles M. Russell, The Life and Legend of America's Cowboy Artist.* Boston: Little, Brown and Company, 1996.

Underwood, Lamar, ed. *Man Eaters—True Tales of Animals Stalking, Mauling, Killing and Eating Human Prey.* Guilford, CT: Lyons Press, 2000.

Index